DUALISM AND DISCONTINUITY
IN INDUSTRIAL SOCIETIES

DUALISM AND DISCONTINUITY IN INDUSTRIAL SOCIETIES

SUZANNE BERGER

Professor of Political Science
Massachusetts Institute of Technology

MICHAEL J. PIORE

Professor of Economics
Massachusetts Institute of Technology

CAMBRIDGE UNIVERSITY PRESS

CAMBRIDGE
LONDON   NEW YORK   NEW ROCHELLE
MELBOURNE   SYDNEY

Published by the Press Syndicate of the University of Cambridge
The Pitt Building, Trumpington Street, Cambridge CB2 1RP
32 East 57th Street, New York, NY 10022, USA
296 Beaconsfield Parade, Middle Park, Melbourne 3206, Australia

First published 1980

Printed in the United States of America
Typeset by The Composing Room of Michigan, Inc., Grand Rapids, Mich.
Printed and bound by The Murray Printing Co., Westford, Mass.

Library of Congress Cataloging in Publication Data
Berger, Suzanne.
Dualism and discontinuity in industrial
societies.

   Bibliography: p.

   Includes index.

   1. Industrialization – Addresses, essays,
lectures.   I. Piore, Michael J., joint author.
II. Title.
HD2326.B46   338.6   79–25172
ISBN 0 521 23134 5

To our teachers, Arne Gronningsater and Stanley Hoffmann

CONTENTS ════════════

PREFACE

This book is the product of a collaboration and of a continuing conversation begun six years ago. Each of the four original participants came from a different academic discipline with research interests that bore no obvious relation to those of the others: Suzanne Berger, a political scientist puzzling over the survival and reproduction of the traditional sector in France and Italy, where modernization should long ago have eliminated all but vestigial traces of traditionalism; Lisa Peattie, an anthropologist concerned with the vitality of the informal sector in the cities of developing countries, when the development literature suggested progressive attrition of this sector; Michael Piore, an economist trying to explain the existence and expansion in several advanced industrial societies of a large labor force of low-skilled workers with insecure jobs and bad pay alongside a labor force with ever more secure and well-remunerated work; and Martin Rein, a sociologist attempting to account for the differential impact of social policy on groups deriving income from various sources. We came to think that these phenomena, variously conceived in our own fields, constituted a single issue for conceptualization. We found as the discussions proceeded that we shared an inchoate sense that the paradigms dominant in our own disciplines were inadequate for interpreting contemporary societies and for generating fruitful new research. These models, for all their differences in subject and scope, converged on the same understanding of industrialization and the nature of industrial society; and this conception and the premises which supported it, we came to feel, was wrong. Ultimately, the conversations seemed to point toward a different way of understanding industrial societies and an alternative conceptualization of the issues with which we had begun.

We hoped to be able to make this new perspective explicit in a single framework of analysis for industrial and industrializing societies, within which each of our separate research enterprises could be seen as a response to questions generated by a common set of problems. Ultimately, this was worked out in only two of the studies and they are the ones presented together in this volume: Berger's on the survival of the traditional sectors of France and Italy, and Piore's on the segmentation of the labor markets of those countries and the United States. These phenomena are elsewhere conceptualized as belonging to separate domains of inquiry. In the perspective developed in this volume, they are shown to lie along a range of alternative solutions to a few common dilemmas that all advanced industrial societies confront: how to distribute economic uncertainty? how to reduce political instability? The small firms, shops, and farms of the traditional sector and dual labor markets are interpreted in our research as structures that have expanded, contracted, and acquired new shape in response to these economic and political problems. We attempt to demonstrate that the apparently anomalous discoveries of the research – the viability of traditional firms, the expansion of dual labor markets – are, in fact, systematic and rational ways in which societies use the material and ideal resources that history and politics make available to resolve current conflicts. In attempting to integrate into this framework the research carried out by Peattie and Rein, we encountered serious difficulties – beyond interesting insights into the similarities of the mechanisms that distribute social goods in various societies – in analyzing the concrete links between the general explanation of industrial societies and the particular research findings of the projects. Though we continue to think that these problems all form part of a single research agenda, we feel this has not yet been sufficiently well demonstrated to justify publishing all four studies together.

Our debts in this enterprise to patrons and colleagues are great. The Ford Foundation generously supported the research through the Center for International Studies at the Massachusetts Institute of Technology. The Center's director, Eugene B. Skolnikoff, offered encouragement and the ear of a friendly critic in the early days. Several of our students participated in the research and developed parallel cases for other societies: Rachid Bademli studied industrial structures in two Turkish cities; Robert Berrier analyzed the survival of traditional firms in the French textile industry; Judith Chubb explored the links between dual labor market structures and political parties in Italy. Adriana Stadecker, Peter Lemieux, and Fabio Basagni contributed to the development of our ideas, as did the students in a seminar we jointly taught in 1974. Our most significant intellectual debt is to our colleagues Lisa Peattie and Martin Rein, with whom we discussed these issues so often and over so long a period of time that their formulations of these questions have undoubtedly entered into the text as our own.

Suzanne Berger
Michael J. Piore

1

OVERVIEW

The two paradigms

Contemporary American economics and political science research have in the main developed out of two distinct but related paradigms. The first one views human behavior and social outcomes as explicable in terms of efforts of individuals to maximize their personal well-being in a competitive environment. Differences in individual outcomes are then explained by differences either in personal preferences or in initial endowments. These in turn are viewed as distributed along a continuum which is reflected in, and used to explain, the distribution of income, power, social status, consumption, and other variables. The second paradigm, that of modernization, attempts to describe the process through which market rationality – and the social structures and political institutions it determines – gain ascendancy. It recognizes the existence of early historical periods in which different behavioral patterns prevailed and explains their disappearance in the process of modernization. The expansion of the market, the spread of communication and of transportation, mass education, and the development of the modern state diffuse a set of rational, maximizing behaviors that are essentially the same for all members of society. The competitive market plays a more or less critical role in various modernization theories. But they all see rationalizing behavior as the force that propels modernization.

Our perspective departs from that inherent in these paradigms at four critical junctures. The first departure from the models dominant in our disciplines arises because they do not systematically account for discontinuities in the behavior of individuals or social classes or in their experiences within the system. To put it simply, the models assume that the rational behavior of individuals maximizing their self-interest generates social and economic structures in which distinctions among individuals and among classes of individuals are con-

1

tinuous. Whether persons are arrayed by income categories or grouped by status, the boundaries or "cutoffs" between one category and the next are essentially arbitrary and a matter of convenience and do not reflect significant real discontinuities. Between the bottom individuals in the ninth decile of an income distribution and the top individuals in the tenth, between the statuses of persons ranked high, medium, and low on a prestige scale, the transitions are smooth and continuous. At the same time, the dominant tendencies of industrial societies – market rationality, modernization – work to diffuse the same socioeconomic structures and, in so doing, integrate all social groupings and economic activities into a society that will be homogeneous in character.

In trying to work on this set of assumptions, each of us had come up against difficulties that threw into question the usefulness of the original paradigm. The societies we were studying seemed far "lumpier" than could be accommodated by any models based on the premise that social and economic structures are generated by continuous variables. The market did not seem to allocate persons and resources, nor did the spread of communication work to diffuse belief, motive, and social structures in the sort of continuous array which either the competition paradigm or the modernization paradigm suggest. The groups we were examining appeared to differ from each other structurally. By this we mean that various segments of society organize around different rules, processes, and institutions that produce different systems of incentives and disincentives to which individuals respond. These "lumps" or social segments are coherent wholes that derive their unity both from the consistency of their internal rules and organization and from the stability of their relationships with other parts of society.

When we began, we called this pattern of social and economic segmentation *dualism*, since the notion evoked both the autonomy of each sector and the radical discontinuities that we were discovering. As we proceeded, it became clear that the significance of dualism is not that a society is divided into *two* autonomous and discontinuous segments but that *a society is divided segmentally and not continuously*. Whether there are two or more such lumps is not central to our conception, though the numbers of segments cannot be multiplied indefinitely without restoring the continuum and returning to the paradigms we have rejected.

The second departure from conventional assumptions arose from the first. Once radical discontinuities are seen as integral features of advanced industrial societies, then the "dualism" that was thought to characterize underdevelopment becomes a point of similarity rather than a distinguishing difference. We thus found ourselves analyzing developed and developing societies in the same frame of reference and were increasingly struck by the similarities between them. For example, whatever the differences – in origin, personnel, and politics – the traditional sector in Italy and the informal sector in Colombia seem to have much in common, and in the former as in the latter case, they perform functions that are critical to the modern sector.

The third basic problem which we encountered as we tried to carry out research on the assumptions of market rationality and modernization centers on the convergence these paradigms appear to predict for all industrial societies. The market rationale and the process through which it imposes itself upon socioeconomic structures and politics should bring industrial countries increasingly to resemble each other and in their similarities to contrast more and more sharply with their own historic antecedents. But if industrialization and modernization do not impose a single behavioral pattern upon society, then the rationale for expecting the same society to emerge in all industrial nations disappears. Since our empirical studies suggested that the number of coherent social and economic segments does vary from society to society, and that this diversity is significant and durable, we found it increasingly less plausible to regard these variations as mere way stations to ultimate convergence.

Finally, in the models of market rationality and modernization, the characteristics of individuals, on the one hand, and their choices and decisions, on the other, determine where individuals will be located in the social structures of modern societies. In contrast, we found that by starting from the premise of groupings that are institutionally defined, we could analyze individual behavior as the response to rules and incentives that develop in different segments of society. Institutions offer rewards and impose constraints upon individuals' actions. These operate in turn to promote certain behaviors and foreclose others. The result is that individuals' choices, attitudes, and behaviors vary across the segments of society. Indeed, if we start from institutions, only a minimal set of assumptions about individuals is required: that the persons found in any particular social and economic universe have at least those predispositions and capabilities that make it possible for them to function there. They may also be capable of operating well in other social segments, and there is no reason to assume a unique mesh between any particular individual's characteristics and his or her social and economic position. Most individuals could probably fit into society at least several different ways. Viewed from this perspective, segmentation and social mobility are in no way incompatible, for where individuals find themselves in society is only minimally accounted for by particular endowments of intelligence, initiative, and appropriate skills.

This perspective suggests that the requirements and constraints of particular institutions are not usually so great as to demand distinctive qualities from members or so compelling as to suffocate in members all predispositions and capacities for participation in some other segment of society. In brief, we can account for social phenomena better by assuming that institutions determine individual responses than by treating social and economic structures as the product of individual behavior. We can account better for individual behavior by looking at the incentives and constraints that prevail in given social groups and by assuming great human plasticity and a wide range of individual possibilities than by starting with a view in which the characteristics of individuals determine their social and economic place.

Explaining segmentation

How can the patterns of segmentation that appear in various industrial societies be explained? Two bodies of theory, by focusing centrally on the discontinuities and heterogeneity of society, seemed most promising for unraveling our puzzle: the literature on economic dualism and Marxist theories of social class. In its earliest version (Boeke), writing on economic dualism conceptualized modern and traditional systems as separate and parallel within a single society: the result of an intrusive modern economic sector which failed to transform the rest of society. Other versions have interpreted dualism as involving an internal restructuring of institutions which maintains a differentiation between a modern sector with advanced technology and capital-intensive enterprise and a traditional sector which is more labor intensive, with smaller enterprise size, local rather than imported technology, and lack of formal education entry requirements. Another version sees the two sectors as the creation of the market. This occurs through "vicious circles" and "backwash effects" that tend to direct profits and investment into a single group of firms which become more and more differentiated from the "backward firms" in factor proportions, market power, wage rates, and employee characteristics. The other sector, starved for resources, is "sickly" and "unhealthy" but never quite dies out.

Some have suggested that the phenomena on which the dualism case is built only show that the process of homogenization has not yet proceeded far enough to integrate society, but that this process will eventually produce the kind of societies that the modernization and market paradigms predict. Yet the evidence from both developed and developing countries suggests the persistence, not the disappearance, of the traditional or informal sector. In fact, much of the traditional sector in developing countries is of recent origin. Even if we argue, therefore, that a single process is working its way through each of these societies, it is not at all clear that this process would in the near future – or perhaps ever – complete the transformation and integration of society. Rather, the evidence from both developing and developed societies suggests that the processes of industrialization and modernization might generate kinds of heterogeneity that would be recast in the old molds.

The notion that industrialization creates forms of social differentiation that are radically distinct from each other and in conflict rather than related by a progressive integration into a seamless social system is at the heart of Marxist theories of modern society. These theories, too, present the advantage – from our perspective – of accounting for individual behavior in terms of institutional location rather than personal qualities, skills, and aptitudes. But we had two difficulties with the conventional Marxist framework. First, as we tried to view the patterns of segmentation we were studying through the lens of class, we found that a significant part of the phenomena we sought to explain fell outside the range of vision. The differentiations within the working class and within the class of capitalists, though acknowledged by Marxists, are not central to their explanatory scheme and, in fact, often must be discussed as problems of "false consciousness" or as transitory divisions that will disappear with the full maturation of capitalism. The relevance of the Marxist enterprise to our own will be discussed later in the volume (see Chapter 5); here we wish simply to note the inadequacy of categories generated by an analysis that grounds the critical social groupings in the dominant mode of production for illuminating the phenomena we set out to explain.

Our second difficulty with the Marxist framework is that it, like the conventional paradigm, seems to imply a convergence of social structures with progressive industrialization whereas, as we began to compare the results of our own research, we were compelled to recognize significant variation among industrial countries and parallels between so-called underdeveloped and developed countries. The notion of a single prototype toward which the process of industrialization inevitably works seemed impossible to sustain.

Views of industrialization

Once we recognized as significant the diverse patterns of segmentation within given industrial societies, the great variations among these societies, and the similarities between underdeveloped and developed societies on precisely those dimensions which we once thought measured development, other questions arose: What remains of the notions of industrialization and modernization? In what sense is it meaningful to think of industrial society at all?

One answer is that these diverse socioeconomic structures are a response to a single set of recurrent problems. In this view, industrialization may be defined in terms of the characteristic problems which it poses for the social structure. To adopt this approach, it is not necessary to have an exhaustive list of what these problems are; in fact, the subsequent essays contain only partial mappings and the lists of problems for each of the essays only partly overlap. Two problems are central to the essays in this volume: political instability and economic uncertainty; the second may be used to illustrate the approach. Instability can be seen as a fundamental problem in all market economies. Piore thus argues that uncertainity, and the way it is handled, is central to the distinction between capital and labor as factors of production. The distribution, or rather, redistribution, of that uncertainity is the underlying issue in the labor market institutions which emerge in response to waves of worker unrest and which appear as the proximate cause of duality in the labor markets of advanced economies.

The ways in which this common problem has been resolved in various societies have produced a range of different socioeconomic structures. The sharpest contrast emerges between the case of Bogotá, which Lisa Peattie studied, and the more advanced industrial nations. In the former, socioeconomic structures reflect the efforts of various groups to build shelters for themselves through local politics and economic actions in a context of overlapping neighborhood economies and clientelist political networks. In the latter, the distribution of insecurity or uncertainty is the subject of national politics. Politics in these countries reflects, reinforces, and generalizes the shelters against uncertainty that groups have conquered and occupied. The political support for such institutions tends, then, to reshape economy and society.

But the similarities among the arrangements in the advanced countries emerge only by contrast with Bogotá. When industrial societies are compared, sharp differences emerge; for example, Italy, where the structures that distribute economic uncertainty rely heavily on a distinction between small and large firms; France, where the structures are dependent on the use of temporary help and migrant workers in large enterprises; and the United States, where both a decentralized pattern of union-management relations and the role of certain ascriptive groups, notably blacks and their relative powerlessness, come into play. These variations are the product of different cultures, different histories, and of critical events that have shaped in distinctive molds the paths of given societies. But there remains in common the single theme to which the variations all respond: in this case, uncertainty.

The *common problems* approach to the definition of industrial society is a kind of minimalist strategy. A more fundamental approach would attempt not only to identify the problems to which the structures of industrial society respond, but also to specify the process which generates those problems. That process, rather than the problems, would then become the defining characteristic of industrialism.

Piore in Chapter 3 does attempt such a conceptualization. The basic process in terms of which industrial society is defined in that essay is the *division of labor,* understood as the fragmentation or the splitting-up of work tasks and productive organizations into increasingly narrower and more distinct components and then the recombination of those components into new, but also more integrated, physical and organizational entities. What fuels this process is pressure to increase output and to produce more goods and services with limited resources. The result of the division of labor is that the process of production becomes more and more specialized, the degree of specialization being limited by the extent of the market.

Instability, viewed from this perspective, is a problem for all industrial societies precisely because it limits the market. The benefits in productive efficiency generated by the division of labor can be appropriated by society only if the specialized productive resources are fully employed. If this is not possible, and the employment of those resources fluctuates widely, then the gains from specialization are dissipated in sustaining the specialized resources in their periods of unemployment, and the productive unit could do better by using a less highly articulated division of labor. This effect tends to lead to a separation of the market for any commodity into a stable component which is met through a relatively extensive division of labor, utilizing highly specialized resources, and an unstable component, where production involves a less highly articulated division of labor, utilizing capital and labor which are less specialized and consequently susceptible to being shifted with fluctuations in demand to other activities.

Thus, we can conceive of the relationship between instability and industrial society in two distinct ways. In one of these, instability and its distribution is a common problem of industrial society and tends to lead to discontinuities in the social structure as groups or as social classes attempt to build shelters against its impact. In the second conception, industrial society is defined by the division of labor, and instability is a variable affecting that process. This view also leads us to expect discontinuities in the socioeconomic structure; these discontinuities are associated with pressures in the system toward economic efficiency and the attempt of producers to separate out a relatively stable and predictable component of demand (where production can utilize the most advanced division of labor) from the fluctuating component of demand, which can be met profitably only with less specialized resources. What the theoretical advantages and difficulties are of the two approaches will be considered in Piore's essay. Here we intend only to signal the presence in the volume of two alternative ways of conceiving the generation of the issues which present themselves on the agenda of industrial societies.

Comparing industrial societies

What is *common* to industrial societies are a set of problems that arise from their technologies; the *differences* among industrial societies are the product of the process through which those problems are resolved. That process is ultimately a political one. In every society what is possible, likely, and desirable is determined by the availability of particular *resources*. These are best imagined as the sum of past values, choices, practices, and institutions out of which can be constructed solutions to the problems of the present. This dependence of the present upon the past has a number of consequences.

The first is that the differences among industrial societies are as significant as their similarities. However powerful the constraints and incentives inherent in the processes and structures of technological change and economic growth, they do not determine a unique set of social, political, or economic arrangements in industrial countries. A very wide range of possible solutions and arrangements have been viable over long periods, and no convergence is in process that will produce a single modal type of industrial society. To show how much the differences matter would require a systematic examination of the impact of various solutions on groups in different societies. There has in fact been substantial research in the past few years on the impact of various solutions to the common problems of industrial societies. It was a foundation program designed to promote such research that financed the work presented in this volume. But however suggestive the idea of functionally equivalent solutions to common problems, it suffers from the same weakness as the modernization paradigm, namely, the notion that at core there is a single type of industrial society and that differences, like those between France and the United States, for example, are less significant and less durable than the similarities. On this assumption, the search for the optimal solution for the common problems is premised. But the nationally specific resources that produce diversity among industrial societies also limit the extent to which solutions worked out in one society might be imported into another. However much flexibility Italy derives from using the traditional sector as a buffer to absorb the economic fluctuations and uncertainties of capitalism, this "solution" is not available to societies lacking a past in which preindustrial groups coalesced around specific constellations of values, social alliances, and institutions into a traditional class of small property holders.

Though the solutions worked out in different societies appear functionally equivalent – in the sense that they seem to solve the same problem – in fact, this equivalence can in no way be prejudged, for solutions may be significantly different in their consequences for the groups that bear the burden and those that reap the rewards of a given outcome. For example, though the Italian traditional sector seems to perform many of the same functions for the economy and polity as the informal sector in Latin American countries, still the ways in which these functions are carried out vary significantly because of the differences among the groups that in Italy inhabit the traditional sector and in Latin America populate the informal sector. In the former case, the owners and workers of the traditional sector benefit from the substantial prestige and political power with which feudalism invested paternalist exercise of power and which early capitalism bestowed on entrepreneurship and private property. The traditional sector in Western Europe draws both on anticapitalist values and on political and social alliances formed in struggles with the feudal regime. From the heritage of these values and from the support of their powerful allies, groups in the traditional sector derive far more prestige than their "functional equivalents" in the Latin American case can command. The solutions represented in different patterns of segmentation thus embody different distributions of risk, influence, and prestige. These solutions also may be better or worse responses to a problem: unemployment in the United States and the use of the traditional sector in Italy differ in their contribution to the problems of inflation and uncertainty.

Finally, the existence of different solutions in different societies confronted by the same problems implies the significance of choice. How national resources are brought to bear on current problems depends in this sense on politics. Whether the dirty, insecure jobs of society are turned over to foreigners, national minorities, or machines does matter, since in each case a different structure of pressures, values, and rewards will shape outcomes for those involved. Even though all of these choices are not available to each society, at least more than one might be.

Implications

As our analysis of industrialism points to the possibility and significance of choice, the normative implications of the essays should be sketched out. These are hardly unambiguous, for they are linked to our focus on the variety of arrangements conceivable in different societies for meeting the same social needs. On the one hand, this perspective brings to the fore the range of alternative resolutions of problems that constrain and limit the satisfaction of human needs in industrial societies. In so doing, it seems to promise an escape from the determinism inherent in the conventional market and modernization paradigms. It would also appear to admit both greater optimism about the impact of social arrangements on individual prospects and a framework for more sophisticated normative judgments than the conventional reliance upon single valued measures of welfare such as income or socioeconomic status.

These promises are in no sense realized in the essays which follow. To begin to do so would require defining the range of possible alternatives; explaining what determines where societies fall in that range; and discovering what they might do to change location. The essays do attempt to account for international variation in the societies we have observed by reference to specific historical experiences out of which industrial institutions grew, cultural context, and particular kinds of politics. This kind of answer, if extended to explain the range of what is possible, leads to a substitution of a cultural and historical determinism for the industrial determinism which we have attempted to escape. To the extent that some extrapolation of this kind is implicit in the logic of the essays, they seem to have conservative implications. But the two questions are in fact quite distinct. To explain why the socioeconomic structure of France differs from Italy or the United States, does not settle the issue of whether alternative structures are possible in France, Italy, or America.

But another problem arises from the very variety in human experiences that we observe in industrial societies. For if this diversity suggests the possibility of change, it makes it very difficult to decide what kind of changes would, in what degree, constitute improvements. We have argued that individuals in industrial societies find themselves, not ranged along a continuum of income or status, but placed within socially structured segments that constitute the settings within which they conduct their affairs. Patterns of behavior develop in adjustment to these settings, and meaning and value come to attach to the behavior and the settings themselves. Since the quality of human experience varies greatly across the segments into which the society and the economy divide, and since it varies critically in ways which are not captured by a single variable like income, life experiences seem virtually incommensurate. Is the self-employed street vendor of Bogotá better or worse off than the industrial worker on the Ford assembly line in Detroit? It is difficult enough to compare the two, let alone decide who is better off.

Does this relativism about the values, attitudes, and expectations that develop in various segments of society oblige us to abandon the search for a normative standard against which the merit of different social arrangements might be held? We believe not: In our perspective, the variations in human behavior and values are explained as responses elicited by different institutions, not as differences intrinsic to the persons who manifest them. In this sense, our work builds on an implicit assumption of a universal human nature, common human needs, and aspirations. We have discovered in the various societies we studied that people are far more adaptable, flexible, and malleable than can be accounted for by theories that root differential outcomes in differential human capabilities. We have been impressed with how easily the skills required for moving from one segment to another are acquired by most people and how little constraining are intrinsic intelligence or initial values and orientations when economic expansion and social change make mobility possible. The same people who once worked in the unstable segment of industry and had poor work habits, little discipline, and low skills move into regular industrial work requiring disciplined, conscientious endeavor when possibilities open for such a shift.

These observations and our research in general are, of course, consistent with two different interpretations: that people are essentially blank blackboards on whom society writes whatever lessons it chooses, as well as the view that there is some fundamental human nature underlying all differences. But no matter which of these two views we adopt, we are obliged to renounce our previous beliefs about the limits of the possible in industrial society and about the range of trade-offs. Much of our pessimism about changing society depends on the belief that the pains of industrial society are a necessary price of its benefits. What is most problematic in this view are not the standards in terms of which we weigh costs and benefits but our beliefs about the limits of the possible. In order to release both imagination and will from the constraints of false necessity, we need a vision of the diverse possibilities that can be realized within industrial societies. The variety of arrangements in existing industrial societies, which our essays display and analyze, cannot be used to define the directions in which our societies should move but only to suggest that alternatives and movement are possible.

PART ONE ══════════════

AN ECONOMIC APPROACH

Theories of dualism arose first in the literature on the economy and society of less-developed countries and appeared as explanations of the development of advanced industrial economies only in the last decade. The dual labor market hypothesis was originally introduced in the United States in the middle 1960s to account for the situation of black workers in Northern central cities. Since then, it has been extended to cover a number of other disadvantaged and underprivileged groups in different national contexts. It has also been related to or incorporated into broader hypotheses about economic dualism, most notably in the size distribution of enterprises and in the economic structure of developing countries. Most of the various notions about dualism were developed independently of each other; relationships among them were perceived only after they had been separately articulated. As the number of related concepts multiplied and their boundaries blurred, the notion of labor market dualism lost much of its analytical power; its present meaning and significance is greatly confused. The project out of which this volume grew provided the occasion to discuss and reformulate these problems The first two chapters are designed to assert the concept of a dual labor market as a distinct analytical construct by developing a series of hypotheses about the origins and nature of dual market structures.

The central hypotheses are two. The first locates the roots of dualism in the flux and uncertainty which adhere in the economic system and in the uneven impact of these parameters of the system upon various factors of production and different groups of workers. The second hypothesis sees dualism as the outgrowth of the process of the division of labor, a process which is in turn understood in terms of a broader view of the nature of industrial development. These two views are developed in the first and second chapters, respectively. The second chapter concludes with a discussion of the broader implications of these processes for an understanding of industrial society.

Before turning to develop the first of these views, some introductory comments are required about the meaning of the term *dualism* in labor market analysis and about why we might be interested in its existence.

The meaning and importance of dualism

The notion of duality in the United States was developed by a group of economists who thought that what they had discovered was fundamentally at odds with the theories which predominated among their colleagues in the profession. They perceived this conflict in various ways: some thought of themselves as institutionalists, others as radicals or Marxists.[1] We shall identify them by the shorthand term *stratification theorists*.

As the debate has evolved, however, a number of orthodox economists have accepted, at least *argumento*, the notion of a dual labor market and have attempted to provide explanations for it that are consistent with conventional theory. In their definition of the problem, what is interesting about the dual labor market hypothesis is the possibility of two different sectors, providing different employment opportunities, with very little mobility between them. The basic empirical question of whether or not there is a dual labor market has been reduced to the question of whether or not there is economic mobility. And the basic analytical question is that of the origins of a dual labor market.[2]

The issues of mobility and origins were not central to the conception of dualism in the view of the stratification theorists, or even to our own early writings on labor markets, however interesting we found these questions for other reasons. The original dual labor market hypothesis was an attempt to capture the structure of the labor market as perceived by the actors within it. For us at the time the different fates of black and white workers in the economy were the critical problem. "Dualism" captured the perception of black workers and of many white workers and employers as well of the structure of differences between black and white employment opportunities. But as the range of research problems has expanded, it became clear that a broader typology was needed, one that expressed discontinuity rather than dualism. What is important about the discontinuities we perceive is that they distinguish labor market segments which are *qualitatively* different. The qualitative differences are such that both the behavioral characteristics of the principal actors (workers and managers) and the nature of human experience vary from one segment to another. Such basic economic processes as wage determination or education and training are fundamentally different in different market segments and cannot be captured by a single model of human behavior. Because the nature of experience is different, well-being of workers in one stratum is fundamentally incommensurate with that of workers in another and cannot be expressed by a single monetary scale. These implications are not pursued very far in the present essays, but they clearly mean that the dualism and discontinuities with which we are concerned would be of interest even if there were substantial mobility across market segments. This understanding of the problem also places rather more stringent requirements on a theory of the "origins" of the market structure, since such a theory must explain not only mobility patterns but also the behavioral differences.

Approaches to dualism

As a result of the different interpretations of the issues posed by the dual labor market hypothesis, several different notions of dualism emerge in the literature. A kind of minimalist notion simply recognizes a distinction between two sectors: a *primary sector*, containing the more attractive and better paying job opportunities, and a *secondary sector*, whose jobs are generally regarded as inferior and less attractive. The disadvantaged and underprivileged groups – originally black workers, but in later versions, ethnic and racial minorities, women, and youth – are confined to the secondary sector. This is the most limited version of the hypothesis. Because what it asserts about the world is so limited, it is consistent with a wide variety of interpretations of how the world operates. For that reason, it is a common point of departure for people with extremely different explanations for the discontinuity whose existence it predicates. The first of the following essays starts from this minimalist notion.

The second essay moves beyond this minimalist approach to a much more comprehensive set of hypotheses about the structure of labor markets. In these the typology of the labor market is more extensive. Three, and for some purposes four, distinct segments or strata are explicitly recognized. Next, the strata are defined in terms of a fairly long list of distinguishing characteristics rather than in terms of a unidimensional index of job quality or the identity of the people who hold them. Both of these first two elements of the definition of labor market structure are, I believe, widely shared among those involved in the original formulation of the hypothesis and reflect the notion that behavior and experience vary across market segments. Finally, the second essay suggests that the list of distinctive behavioral characteristics which define the strata are generated by a single, basic, underlying difference, that is, a difference in the way in which people learn, and subsequently understand, the work which they perform. This explanation would probably not be generally acceptable to dual or stratification theorists, but it is central to the argument developed below.

The segments of the labor market recognized in the second essay are, in addition to the secondary sector, a primary sector divided into an *upper* and a *lower* tier.[3] The upper tier consists of professional and managerial employment. The lower tier includes jobs generally termed "blue collar" or "working class" as well as certain ones that are "white collar." Intermediate between the upper and lower tiers of the primary sector are a set of jobs referred to in the United States as the "crafts," which are difficult to classify because they share characteristics of both strata.

Secondary work situations are characterized by relatively low wages, poor working conditions, and generally inferior or demeaning social status. The jobs provide little security or career advancement. They are essentially unskilled, either requiring no skill at all, or utilizing basic human skills and capacities shared by virtually all adult workers. A highly personal relationship often prevails between workers and supervision, unmediated by formal work rules or procedural due process for the review of authority. Wages tend to be determined either directly or indirectly by statute. The labor force in these jobs is composed of distinct groups who derive their principal identity from social roles outside the work place: women, adolescents, peasant workers, or temporary migrants. Such workers are typically unstable, with a high rate of voluntary turnover, and frequent movement in and out of the labor force.

The lower tier of the primary sector, by contrast, constitutes a far more stable work environment. The jobs are better paying, with generally less unpleasant working conditions and greater social status. They typically provide considerable security, a certain opportunity for advancement toward higher wages, and more attractive opportunities over the course of a work life. The jobs are relatively skilled, but most of the skills are acquired on the job in the process of production with workers learning from one another. Formal classroom instruction prior to employment is relatively unimportant in the skill acquisition process. The situation lends itself to the formation of stable social groups within the work place, and the relationship between worker and supervisor tends to be mediated either by such informal groups or by more formal union organizations. Work and authority are, as a result, governed by custom and formal rules and procedures, and the exercise of authority is frequently subject to a

review process. Wages are usually set through collective bargaining
or through informal procedures which resemble the formal bargaining process and conform to a set of norms governing the relationship
among wage rates of various jobs in the shop and between the shop
and external points of reference.

The upper tier of the labor market is composed of professional and
managerial jobs. These jobs stand at the top of the hierarchy in terms
of pay, status, and prestige. They generally provide substantial job
security and offer more extensive opportunities for career advancement over a wider geographic area and a broader range of institutions
than the jobs in the lower tier. Typically, they involve formal education prior to employment. The work group and the work community
in the upper tier is less cohesive. The customs and rules governing
work in the upper tier are considerably less important, and internalized codes of behavior substitute for both these rules and for the
personal supervision common in the secondary sector.

Intermediate between the upper and lower tier of the labor market
are a series of craft jobs difficult to classify. The jobs resemble those of
the lower tier in that skills are acquired on the job in the process of
production and the work group and customs seem extremely important in the learning process and in the day-to-day relationship among
workers and between workers and supervisors. But many craftsmen
develop an independence which more closely resembles that characteristic of professionals and managers. Their geographic and institutional mobility is sometimes closer to that of workers in the upper tier
as well. And while formal instruction is not generally important in
initial job preparation, it is very often used to supplement on-the-job
training after the latter is under way or substantially complete.

The differences among strata appear to be explicable in terms of the
ways in which people learn and understand their work. From this
point of view, we can distinguish two learning processes. In one,
people learn an abstract concept and, when faced with a concrete
work operation, deduce from it how to perform the job. Thus, for
example, in the assembly of an automobile, workmen might acquire a
mental picture of a car and the rudimentary principles governing its
operation. When presented with an assortment of parts, they could
then figure out how to put it together. Learning of this kind may be
termed *abstract* learning and the understanding to which it leads is
intrinsic understanding.

The alternative form of learning may be termed *concrete* or *extrinsic*. In this case, people learn the particular operations directly and
then mentally organize them in relation to *spaces* which are external
or extrinsic to the operations themselves, for example, in relation to a

time sequence or to the physical or social setting in which the operations are performed. Thus, in the case of car assembly, the alternative to "figuring out" how to build a car, is to memorize a sequence of operations which can then be performed by rote. Workers on the automobile assembly line seem to understand their jobs in this way. The "external" space in terms of which the operations are understood and fixed in the mind are provided by time. In other jobs, people learn to perform an operation in response to a physical cue such as a light on a board or the color produced by a chemical reaction in a process. In still other situations, the space is *social*, the behavior of a customer in a restaurant might produce a particular response on the part of the waiter: signals from other workers provide clues for work operations in complex manufacturing jobs in the way that a light on a board does in simpler ones.

The distinctive characteristics of the upper and lower tiers may be attributed to the difference between abstract and concrete learning. The lower tier is characterized by concrete learning. That type of learning explains the importance of on-the-job training: Concrete learning requires the display of the specific operations involved in the context in which they will be performed. Abstract learning, which characterizes the upper tier, can, in contrast, occur in an environment removed from the actual work situation; hence, the role of the formal classroom in learning in the upper tier. By the same token, abstract learning seems to permit greater geographic and institutional mobility than concrete learning, since in the latter knowledge is contingent upon stability in the external environment. This explains the difference in mobility patterns and careers in the two tiers of the primary sector. The importance of stability also helps explain the role of the work groups in the lower tier: The external social structure is one of the "spaces" in terms of which the concrete knowledge is organized and understood; this space is not so important in the upper tiers because work depends on abstractions which are not specific to a particular social setting. The different relationships among workers and between worker and supervisor in the two strata may also be seen as a reflection of the different types of learning: The internalized codes of behavior which govern relationships in the upper tier are essentially analogous to the abstract understandings which govern work operations; the rules and customs which govern in the lower tier are basically the same as the *concrete* understanding of work operations.

The craft jobs which appear to lie between the two tiers can also be understood in these terms; craftsmen learn concrete operations on the job, and in this sense craft work situations are like those of the lower tier. But the range of operations which a craftsman must master are typically much wider than those mastered by other workers through on-the-job learning. The range permits some craftsmen to perceive the underlying principles which govern the relationships among the various tasks they have learned to perform and, once they have done so, they are able to operate on the basis of these rules, using abstractions in a manner similar to that in which upper tier workers figure out how to perform tasks they have not previously encountered.

When the primary sector is interpreted in this way, the salient characteristic of the secondary sector becomes the impossibility of perceiving the work performed there in any coherent way at all. Except for the simplest assembly, the operations are so unstable that they are difficult to memorize at all. But, at the same time, the tasks are often so diverse and the workers so far removed from the forces which are generating that diversity that it is impossible to perceive the principles underlying these work operations. Fortunately, the work is essentially unskilled, that is, does not require any real understanding on the part of those who perform it. Because they do not understand the work in its own terms, however, the workers are incapable either of initiating or coordinating their activity, and it is for this reason that the personal direction of the supervisor becomes a central factor in the work situation.

Once the various strata of the labor market are understood in this way, the central theoretical task becomes that of explaining what determines the way in which work is learned and understood. The second chapter is directed toward this task. We turn first, however, to the simpler task of explaining the origins of *duality*, that is, the distinction between a primary and a secondary sector. As noted, the definition of dualism required for this initial task is a much more elemental distinction between "good" and "bad" jobs.

Notes

1. For a summary of these early views, see David Gordon, *Theories of Poverty and Underemployment* (Lexington, Mass.: D.C. Heath, 1972).
2. Glen C. Cain, "The Challenge of Segmented Labor Market Theories to Orthodox Theories: A Survey," *Journal of Economic Literature, 14* (December 1976), no. 4, 1215–59; and Michael Wachter, "The Primary and Secondary Labor Market Mechanism: A Critique of the Dual Approach," *Brookings Papers on Economic Activity* (1974) no. 3, 637–80.
3. Gordon, Reich, and Edwards use the terms *independent* and *subordinate* spheres for what I am calling here the "upper" and "lower" tier. See

Michael Reich, David Gordon, and Richard C. Edwards, "A Theory of Labor Market Segmentation," in Gerald Somers (ed.), *Proceedings of the Twenty-Fifth Anniversary Meeting, December 28–9, 1972, Toronto* (Madison, Wis.: Industrial Relations Research Association, 1973), p. 270.

2

DUALISM AS A RESPONSE TO FLUX AND UNCERTAINTY

The principal line of argument developed in this essay is that dualism in the labor market is at root connected to the variability and uncertainty of modern, industrial economies. Historically, the labor force has been used to resolve the problems which these economies generate for the productive process. This has been true in the relatively banal sense that labor is the variable factor of production and, as such, can be freely hired and fired as productive activity fluctuates. In this respect, it contrasts to the fixed factor, capital (or more concretely, plant and equipment), which cannot be forced to bear the cost of its own unemployment. This difference has led employers to be more careful in their planning for capital equipment utilization and to confine fluctuations, as much as possible, to sectors of the economy (and to productive units within particular industries) which are intensive in labor. But it is also true in a second sense: labor is treated as the residual variable in planning and engineering. These processes in modern industrial society are essentially sequential (rather than simultaneous or iterative). One aspect of a plan or engineering design is completed before an attempt is made to resolve the next. The labor component is generally the last factor which is taken into account, virtually forcing the labor force to adjust to other aspects of the economic system rather than the other way around.[1]

In the following chapter, we will suggest that labor may constitute a residual factor of production in still a third sense. The basic argument presented there is that technological progress consists in dividing up the productive process into its component parts and then attaching those components one by one to other operations where they are governed by a different and presumably more efficient logic. In this process of segregating out operations and assigning them elsewhere, a residue of older operations which cannot, or cannot yet, be reassigned is left behind. The residual appears increasingly diffuse and heterogeneous as more and more of the components which once linked related operations and gave them coherence and meaning are removed. And labor is capable of performing these residual tasks in a way that capital equipment generally cannot, for the latter must incorporate the tasks into its own logic. Workers, on the other hand, can operate by rote or can simply be told what to do and need themselves have no logical understanding of the relationships among tasks at all.

These contrasts between the treatment of labor and capital in production planning suggest that the *original* dualism in modern economies is between *labor* and *capital*. Dualism within the labor market arises when portions of the labor force begin to be insulated from uncertainty and variability in demand and their requirements begin to be anticipated in the process of planning and decision making. They become at this point like capital, and the original dualism between capital and labor becomes a duality between that portion of the labor force which shares in some part the privileged position of capital and those other workers who continue to function as the "residual" factor of production. This accounts for the observation at the origin of interest in the dual labor market: that it is a distinction between privileged and underprivileged positions in the socioeconomic structure.

There is one respect, however, in which the other view of dualism, as defined by qualitative behavior differences, is relevant to the present context. Once a distinction is made in the labor market by the effort to deal with flux, and a labor force called into being to absorb the insecure portion of demand, that labor force may also be used to handle other social functions. To the extent that the two sectors are distinguished by their behavior patterns, jobs may fall into one or another sector – not because the jobs are more or less secure, but because the behavioral patterns differ. Thus, when we look at the labor market at any moment (i.e., using a static, behavioral analysis) there will be certain jobs (e.g., hospital orderly) that are in the secondary labor market although demand seems perfectly stable, and other jobs (in the United States, most construction jobs constitute such examples), which we would call primary despite considerable fluctuation in demand. This, however, need not detract from the assertion that it is the attempt to handle flux that calls into being the distinction between the two sectors and frustrates attempts to eliminate it.

The causes of duality

Four principal reasons are advanced in the literature for the development of the distinctions among different types of jobs which give rise to dualism. First, it is argued that employers have an incentive to treat workers like capital when they have invested in the worker's training. Workers then become a "quasi-fixed factor" of production or *quasi capital*.[2] This point has been developed most recently in theoretical terms by the human capital school of economics, but it is a point central to an earlier literature about "labor force commitment" in underdeveloped economies and is one of the leading explanations of economic dualism in Japan. It implies that duality arises in a capitalist economy because such duality is "efficient": it would tend to maximize the product in a static economy and in a developing economy it contributes to economic growth. A second explanation for duality in the labor market is that it is forced upon the employer by the efforts of certain groups to escape their position as a residual factor and to secure their jobs. It thus tends to be associated with trade union organization and activity imposing restrictions directly upon the employer through collective activity at the work place or through the legislative and political process.[3] A third explanation, closely related to the second, sees duality as the outgrowth of the national employment contract between workers and their employers in which the latter, in return for certain concessions in the level of wages, agree to stabilize the variability of wages and employment. This explanation in terms of an implicit rational contract assumes a certain asymmetry in the attitude toward risk on the part of workers and employers which could result either from inherent differences in risk preferences or from access to institutional mechanisms for insuring against, or shifting the burden of risk.[4] Finally, a fourth explanation is that duality results from efforts on the part of employers to divide what would otherwise be a united working class and stave off the revolution. This view of duality emphasizes its role in the broader class struggle and has been developed by Marxists and by radical economists and is most widely accepted among them.[5]

Other possible explanations of duality relate some accidental association between particular workers and some favored places within the economic system, as a complement to capital equipment, for example, or in some sector of the economy whose demand is particularly stable. These explanations have not, however, been prominent in the literature on dualism, nor are they very rich analytically. They do not figure in the argument that follows.

All these explanations identify the principal cause of economic dualism in the organization of production on the demand side of the market and, in the last three versions, among the workers of the primary labor force. We must also explain why the jobs in the secondary sector are concentrated among certain groups of workers rather than others. This is an especially important part of the analysis when, as in the case here, we are interested in disadvantaged workers. Our conclusions depend in great measure upon which explanation of the demand side of the market seems the most compelling. In general, the human capital explanation tends to emphasize the relative "trainability" of different groups of workers and their stability, or attachment to the enterprise, once trained. The other explanations tend to emphasize the political and economic power of various different groups of workers: the secondary workers are economically and politically weak. The second and third explanations also suggest the importance of differences among workers in the strength of their dislike for the instability and uncertainty inherent in the secondary sector. Certain groups of workers, such as married women, youth, and temporary migrants, with a relatively weak job attachment and other, nonwork-related interests, may find these characteristics less disturbing than primary wage earners.

With this last class of explanations (i.e., those emphasizing the weak job or labor market attachment of secondary workers), an important distinction should be drawn between those who see such an attachment as a product of the system itself and those who see it as a largely exogenous factor. In the latter view, which is developed in Berger's essays in this volume, the particular characteristics of secondary workers are largely "accidents" which the economic system makes use of but which it does not create. In the former view, sex roles, racism, ethnicity, youth, and the like, are categories which, if not actually created by employers, have at the very least been vastly strengthened and manipulated by them in order to stabilize and legitimize the economic structure.

Historical development

To understand the historical development of labor market duality and evaluate its policy implications, it is important to distinguish between the analysis of particular labor markets and industries (the microeconomic level) and dualism in the national labor market. Given any particular labor market, it is usually possible to identify a cleavage between stable and unstable (secure and insecure) employment which meets our definition of duality. Roger Cornu, for example, found such a duality *within* mining in France, an industry previously taken as the paradigm of a stable, fixed labor force.[6] The division in the mines lay between a permanent labor force composed of skilled adult men and an unskilled, variable work force composed of women, youth who had not yet completed their military service (and whom managerial authority and social pressure discouraged from marrying), part-time peasant workers, and foreign workers. In the mines, this distinction apparently derived from management's need to maintain a trained labor force (i.e., to conserve specific human capital); it might also be interpreted as a means of managerial control. Lisa Peattie found dualities in Bogotá *within* what previous observers had termed the secondary labor market: for example, the distinction between street vendors who are licensed vendors with permanent and preferred positions and itinerant unlicensed vendors.[7] This distinction reflects, at least in some measure, the pressure of the work force in the licensed sector to maintain the stability of its income, but it is also an accidental by-product of efforts of middle-class planners to impose the order which they see as part of civilized urban society.

Other examples of dualistic labor market structures on the microlevel include Brody's description of the preunion steel industry in the United States,[8] studies conducted by Paci in Northern and Central Italy,[9] in France the Destefanis–Vasseur study of the Annecy labor market,[10] Berrier's study of the French textile industry,[11] and Magaud's on temporary and permanent employment in the public sector.[12]

Taken together, what these particular microstudies reveal is an immense variety both in the institutional arrangements which separate secure from insecure employment and in the types of workers which are found to accept the insecure jobs. They also seem to suggest that the various theories of dualism are not mutually exclusive. Their explanatory power varies from one situation to another, but examples can be found where each is operative; sometimes they operate together and are mutually reinforcing. The microstudies also show that there are dualisms within dualisms: Separate a group of insecure jobs from others and that group is often subdivided again into two groups, one of which is relatively more secure.

All of this is still consistent with our original notion of economic dualism: The structuring of the market is in each case a response to the conflict between the inherent insecurity in the economic activity and pressures (either narrowly economic or of a broader social and political character) for protection and security. Viewed from a macroperspective, all of these dualistic markets lie along a continuum of arrangements in terms of the overall degree of security which they provide. But at the microlevel a dichotomy emerges, created by the attempt to resolve the problem through dichotomous institutional arrangements. In each case the secondary labor force (the women in mining, the unlicensed vendors in Bogotá) is a genuinely underprivileged group, deserving of policy concern. Still, as long as dual-

28   *An economic approach*

ism exists solely on the microlevel, its value is questionable as either
an analytical construct or an instrument of policy analysis. To solve
whatever problems such microdualism creates, we have to worry
about highly specific arrangements: the mining industry and its
women; the vendors and their licenses. To know that these people
are part of a dualistic structure in their own industry or market may be
interesting, but not very helpful for policy.

Recently, attention has focused not on microeconomic dualism in
particular labor markets, but on the extensions of dualism throughout
the national economy. Macroeconomic dualism of this kind arises
when there is a broad similarity across most if not all of the economy –
first, in the pressures for a division between secure and insecure jobs;
next, in the particular institutions through which the division is created and maintained; and finally, in the groups which are found to man
the insecure sector. These extensions can be seen by a brief review of
the dual labor market in three countries where it has been the subject
of considerable recent research: Italy, France, and the United States.

Italy

The clearest case of labor market dualism in the industrialized West is
presented by Italy.[13] The Italians themselves perceive their economic
structure in this way, and this makes dualism the "conventional wisdom." Elsewhere the structure of the labor market may be equally
dualistic, but is perceived in these terms if at all only by a relatively
small group of analysts, often of a particular political persuasion.[14]
Italian dualism cannot be understood simply by analyzing labor markets. The research Suzanne Berger presents in Chapter 4 on the role of
traditional enterprises in Italy and on the political and social
functions of dualism shows that the segmentation of the labor force is
only one part of a larger phenomenon whose origins and supports are
fundamentally political. This section, then, should be read together
with her account of the broad context within which dualism has developed in postwar Italy, in order to understand how the segmentation of the labor force and of firms emerged alongside the dualism
that Italians traditionally had identified as the distinguishing feature
of their society – the geographic one between the developed industrial North and the relatively underdeveloped rural South.[15]

In the current conventional wisdom of the Italians, the dichotomy
in the structure of the labor market was powerfully reinforced, though
not created, by the "hot autumn" of 1969 and the changing attitudes
and institutional forms that flowed from that episode. Prior to 1969,
the postwar Italian labor movement had been relatively weak and,

particularly at the shop level, ineffectual. The work place had in the immediate aftermath of World War I been the scene of active class struggle, conducted through elaborate shop-level organizations by a militant rank and file. This structure required continuous negotiation and accommodation between labor and management on issues relating directly to production itself. That organization had been suppressed by Mussolini and was unable to reassert itself in the immediate postwar period.[16] Throughout most of the postwar period the arena of class struggle was party politics. The labor movement itself was sharply divided among Christian, communist, and socialist organizations, each of which was closely allied with, and to a great extent dominated by, their respective political parties. The unions negotiated basic wage agreements on an industry or company level but were not active in the shop. And, indeed, the docility of the labor movement was often credited with the Italian economic miracle, the rapid rates of economic growth in the early sixties and the unique price stability of that decade and the one which preceded it.

The fall of 1969 was a distinct rupture in the apparent harmony of social relations generally and productive relations in particular. A massive wave of wildcat strikes, sit-downs, and "occupations" broke out in work places and universities throughout Italy. The strikes were apparently a spontaneous expression of accumulated and suppressed discontents, an open-ended protest as opposed to a strategic, programmatic campaign. The workers freely allied themselves with the students and borrowed from the latter a vocabulary and an ideology which were genuinely shocking to the disciplined cadres of the organized political left, to whom this appeared often as irresponsible anarchism, childish and adventuristic. It placed the initial industrial protest outside the existing institutional structure of both the labor movement and the political parties.

The intensity of the initial protest abated somewhat in the winter of 1969, but the movement which it initiated and the spirit which it evoked continued; indeed, to a certain extent it has become a permanent feature of the Italian social scene. While preserving a good deal of its spontaneity, and much of the accompanying anarchy and unpredictability as well, however, the worker movement which grew out of the fall of 1969 has gradually been institutionalized. Probably the most important aspect of that institutionalization has been the development of shop-level worker councils encompassing the protest movement but built into preexisting union organizations. In a sense, this is a revival of institutional forms prevalent in Italy in the interwar period and suppressed under fascism.[17] They have been strengthened by a major legislative reform – *il statuto del lavoro* – modeled on the

American system of industrial relations which protects the right of workers to organize, especially at the shop level. The net effect of these changes has been to give the labor movement, particularly in large plants, a new independent base. The unions used that base to move away from their previous reliance upon the political parties and toward increasing cooperation among the separate union organizations.

In labor management relations, the new institutional forms have meant a shift from high-level negotiations over general wage rates to much broader negotiations at the plant and shop level, encompassing the widest possible range of issues surrounding production and work. It is important to appreciate exactly how wide and, in a sense, unrestricted that range of issues is, covering questions of discipline, promotion, discharge, and work allocation with which American trade unions have traditionally concerned themselves but which have not been subjects of collective bargaining in Western Europe. Negotiations also extend to the actual technology and content of production and work, considered not simply in the context, or as an extension, of concerns about discipline and job security but as an issue that should be evaluated in its own right in terms of the job satisfaction and alienation of the workers.[18] The range of negotiable issues has also extended in the other direction to include the role of the company, directly and indirectly, in broader social and economic policy. For example, Fiat was forced to agree to a contract which committed it to policies for transportation, housing, and regional development which affected groups of workers extending well beyond its own employees. Unions here have, moreover, pressed for things seldom demanded by American unions: escalator clauses tying all wages to price indices; wage differentials; unified wage setting procedures and lines of career advance for blue and white collar jobs.

These negotiations can be interpreted in various ways, and in fact, there is no consensus on their significance in Italy today. From the point of view of the labor movement itself, the content is seen as an attempt to preserve and develop the spirit of the worker movement of 1969 and, in particular, its spontaneous translation of often inarticulate grievances against the industrial system into operational goals.

Both unions and parties of the left refer to the workers' councils of the twenties to understand and legitimate the new forms of factory organization. This approach has enabled the established union organizations to assimilate a basically anarchistic movement and to utilize that movement to gain increasing independence from the political parties upon which they were previously dependent. It has also enabled the orthodox Communist Party to identify with a social movement which began beyond its reach and has continually threatened to outflank the party on the left. There has been a price for all of this. The party has lost much of its control over the unions; and both the party and the unions, by legitimizing the spontaneous and unpredictable characteristics of worker protest, have probably also exaggerated them.

Employers, not surprisingly, see these developments in a very different light. For them, the evolution of the labor movement since 1969 represents a rigidification of the productive process. The increasing militancy and power of the workers in the shop, the sanctification of that power through government legislation, the refusal of the institutionalized labor movement to restrain and control that power, its insistence instead on glorifying and legitimizing the very characteristics which make protest erratic and unpredictable, and the attempt to translate demands which initially expressed themselves in extreme obstinacy on the part of individual workers into far-reaching changes in the productive structure within the shop and the social structure outside it – all imply a loss of control over the productive process. Prior to 1969, there were certain basic restrictions upon management's prerogatives. There were general limitations upon discipline, and extensive severance pay provisions inhibited layoff and discharge. After 1969, management seems to have lost the possibility to suspend or discharge workers at all. It came to feel itself unable to discipline workers for absence, tardiness, or infractions of work rules and unable to lay off workers in response to variations in demand. In addition, employers felt that through the introduction of automatic wage escalators, the collapse of wage differentials and the changes in job classification schemes, they had lost control over the wage level and the ability to utilize the wage structure to motivate and control work.[19]

The response of management to this rigidification has been an effort to restore its flexibility by transferring productive activity to a secondary sector. The roots of the secondary sector in Italy and its symbiotic relationship to the rest of the productive structure can be traced to the immediate postwar period. The traditional working class and its organizations, which had led the opposition to fascism, emerged from the war in an aggressive, militant mood, tightly organized at the grass roots level for both economic and political action; they used their power to press for gains, both through contractual and legal provisions. Employers responded to these pressures by seeking to evade existing obligations and to break the power which had imposed them. For these purposes, they developed a system of supplementing production by the customary industrial labor force with women, peasant workers, and migrants from the South, employing them either in small enterprises which were more difficult to organize, at home under the putting-out system, or under special institutional arrangements which segregated them from other workers and barred them from access to the rights the prime labor force had won.[20]

Ultimately, these tactics and even more important, repression of unions within the big plants were successful in breaking the power of the organized working class and restoring a climate more favorable to employers within the productive apparatus. As a result, Paci argues, in the years of the Italian economic miracle (1958–63), the locus of expansion shifted back into the primary sector and the tendency was to absorb into that sector the marginal industrial workers who, in the preceding period, had been maintained in segregated institutions. The secondary sector declined. The miracle was followed in 1963 by a severe industrial depression, but the labor market patterns of the miracle years continued to prevail in the sense that employers reacted to the depression by expelling the marginal work force and concentrating production in large units and employment in a core force of industrial workers.[21]

After 1969, however, shifts in employment back towards the secondary sector gained increasing importance, as the research Berger reports here and elsewhere shows.[22] The critical mechanisms that operate in the secondary sector reduce union power and lower labor costs.[23] First, certain firms are exempted, by size, from major pieces of labor legislation. For example, the labor law guaranteeing the right of plant organization does not apply to units with less than sixteen employees. Controls on dismissal for redundancy do not apply to firms with less than ten employees. Artisanal firms operate under special labor regulations and receive special treatment from banks, the tax system, and the social security system. Thus, small firms not only escape from many of the fixed labor costs of larger enterprises but also pay lower wages. (The significant wage differentials within industrial sectors according to firm dimensions are presented in Table 4; see Chapter 4, on the uses of the traditional sector.) Smaller firms have greater flexibility in the use of labor as well.[24]

The distinguishing feature of firms in this component of the secondary sector is that they operate within a distinct legal regime. The second component of the Italian secondary sector operates outside the existing legal framework and forms a kind of gray or black market. The extreme form of this is *lavoro a domicilio*, essentially a revival of the putting-out system in which production is let out by contractors to be performed by people in their homes.[25] The labor force for these smaller enterprises is drawn from a variety of marginal groups. Some people employed in this way are genuinely underprivileged industrial workers, are too weak to organize and unable to gain access to more favorable employment. In the Milan area, for example, Paci argues that this labor force is heavily dominated by women, youth, and the aged, who were driven out of the better employment opportunities in the 1960s by the massive migration of prime-age, male workers from the South.[26] But, in other cases, the work force in this secondary labor market is composed of people who obtain the economic and social security provided in large enterprises in other ways. Among these other ways are peasant workers in the North who maintain a small plot of land which supplements their income when they are working, will sustain them for some period of time when they are laid off, and which may be sufficient to support them in their old age when their children are grown. Another group are recent migrants from the South whose family and landholdings back home provide a similar cushion against adversity. For still other workers, the cushion against adversity comes from the primary sector itself. The workers are wives and children of men who work in large enterprises and derive economic security and medical protection for themselves and their children from that source. It is widely alleged that the skilled labor in these small enterprises is composed of actual employees from the large enterprises, some of whom are moonlighting and some of whom constitute the absentees that management in the large companies has lost the ability to discipline and control.

France

A story can be told about dualism in France which parallels the Italian story, although this view of the labor market is nowhere near as widespread among the French themselves as it is among the Italians, and the institutional structure of the two sectors is indeed very different. The French analog to the "hot fall" of 1969 is May 1968. The "events" of May and June began in the university with student strikes and demonstrations. This unrest spread to the factories, where it produced a wave of sit-down strikes and culminated in a general strike, which brought the economy to a standstill. The strikes were settled and production and order restored by a negotiated settlement between labor and management known as the *accords de Grenelle*.

The basic outcome of 1968 was a heightened sensitivity on the part of employers to the possibility of worker resistance to their assigned role in the productive process in general and to economic layoffs in particular. The social protest, apparently coming out of nowhere, revealing an unsuspected depth of dissatisfaction, and demonstrating the inherent fragility of the social structure, shocked both labor and management and altered their perspectives of themselves and each other and of what was possible and desirable in the evolution of French society. What was created by 1968 was thus a heightened awareness of the impact of the organization of the productive process on the human sensibilities of the labor force. The lessons of 1968 itself have been reenforced in the post-1968 period by a series of lesser strikes and sit-downs, of which the most prominent was the lengthy and highly publicized occupation of the Lip watch factory, in which the workers resisted a plant closing by occupying the facility and continuing the production and marketing of the product.

The year 1968 also led to specific reforms which created institutional restraints upon the employer's capacity to deploy his work force in the customary manner. These reforms were presaged by the *accords de Grenelle,* which ended the general strike and were later implemented through detailed labor-management agreements. Subsequently, the reforms were reenforced and extended by legislation. That legislation has, in turn, been amended and strengthened at several critical junctions.

The important institutional reforms are twofold: first, increased administrative restraints upon the employer's freedom to lay off or discharge workers for economic (as opposed to disciplinary) reasons; and second, the right of the work force to organize in the work place itself and, once organized, to work through their representatives in the shop to oversee and restrain managerial action. Administrative restraints upon layoff and discharge had existed in France since 1945. They were exercised through the *inspecteur du travail* whom employers were required to notify in the case of "collective layoffs." The *inspecteurs,* in turn, were empowered to use the administrative process to delay, review, and arguably to prevent the employer's proposed actions. Their capacity to curtail discharge, however, deteriorated throughout the 1950s; tentative efforts were made to strengthen administrative control in the early 1960s but were not very successful. In the *accords de Grenelle* employers agreed in principle to the reestablishment of the restraints which administrative control implied. And this, combined with a series of changes in procedures and in statutory language, has created a climate in which it is much easier for the *inspecteurs du travail* to exercise restraint and consequently much harder for employers to utilize layoffs to absorb economic variability. It is impossible to lay off permanent employees quickly and easily, and very large employers in areas where the work force is well organized and militant may find that for practical purposes it is too expensive to try to do so at all.[27]

The second major institutional reform permitted union organization within the shop. Prior to 1968, worker representatives in the shop were kinds of shop stewards (*délégué du personnel*) in units of more than ten workers, and in units of more than fifty, plant committees (*comité d'entreprise*). The former were concerned with enforcing individual legal rights within the shop and, without the backing of a larger organization, had limited effect. The latter were envisaged as vehicles for labor-management cooperation and discussed matters of common interest. Unions and union organizers were completely excluded from the enterprise itself and genuine labor negotiations generally involved common industrial issues, not the specific problems of individual work places.

The events of 1968 substantially altered this pattern. Spontaneous worker groups sprung up in firms throughout France. Initially these groups were not closely connected with the major national unions. But the groups gave to the strike movement what organizational structure it had. The capacity to bring the strikes to an end through national negotiations depended upon the ability of the unions in those negotiations to represent these plant-level groups and become their spokesmen. It ultimately depended as well on the capacity to supplement a national agreement with local understandings dealing with the particular grievances of these shop-level groups. The institutional reforms which followed made the best of a de facto situation by incorporating an essentially wildcat labor movement within existing labor organizations. The reforms gave the unions the right to engage in active organizing in the shop through such activities as pamphleteering, talking to workers, and holding meetings; they created a new plant-level position, union representative; they gave the unions the right to put up candidates for the *comité d'entreprise*; and they allowed for plant-level collective agreements.[28]

The effect of these reforms, and of the general political and social climate which produced them, has been a decrease, keenly felt by employers, in their freedom to deploy labor in the accustomed manner or, in the words which management is more likely to use, in a rigidification of the labor force. But the reforms have not operated in quite the manner which the legal changes, taken at face value, would seem to suggest. The actual impact of the reforms has been very uneven, with considerable variation across the French productive structure in the degree of so-called rigidification. The result has been that employers in the more rigid sectors have sought, more or less successfully, to transfer demand – or at least that portion requiring flexibility – to the less rigid sectors. It is from these efforts that the duality in the French labor market arises.

Four factors are chiefly responsible for the uneven impact of 1968 and its aftermath upon labor utilization. First, the administrative control over layoffs exercised by the *inspecteurs du travail* is very responsive to the local political and social climate. Where the work force is well organized and militant, the *inspecteur* is prone to delay layoffs and attempts to negotiate with employers to preserve the work force. Where the work force is more acquiescent, however, the *inspecteur* tends to be more accommodating. This is inevitable, given the ambiguity of the legislation, the discretion it allows the *inspecteur*, and the nature of the political and bureaucratic climate in which discretion is exercised. But we can also argue that it is consistent with the preeminent aim of the administrative control: to preserve social stability in a climate of class antagonism by balancing the requirements of the productive system against the dangers of anarchy and revolution which 1968 had raised.

Second, there is indeed wide variation in the degree of organization and militancy of different groups within the French labor force. As a rule, workers have been more docile in the traditional, rural, agricultural areas than in older centers of industrialization. Foreign workers have been less militant than native workers, women less militant than men. These differences remain despite the fact that since 1968 previously nonmilitant groups have become more active.

Third, the institutional reforms left several specific exemptions. The reforms applied to permanent workers; temporary workers were covered neither by the restrictions upon layoffs nor by the provisions for plant-level representation. Also exempted from plant-level representation are establishments of less than fifty employees.

Fourth, employers appear to have been quite successful in restraining plant organization in plants of fifty to one hundred employees and even in somewhat larger productive units. Plants in this middle range do not generally have union representation or plant-level agreements,[29] and unions have not achieved representation on the *comités d'entreprise*. Indeed, the latter appear to be utilized increasingly by employers as a vehicle for the traditional paternalistic style of industrial relations and as an alternative to the reforms envisaged in 1968.[30] Thus, insofar as the rigidification is a product of increased worker organization in the shop, it characterizes primarily large enterprises.

It would take us too far afield to explore in any detail why this has been the case. But it should be noted that much of this spontaneous organization which sprang up in May 1968 receded in its wake, providing employers an opportunity to reassert traditional managerial styles. The regular union movement, on the other hand, has always been ambivalent about work place organization of this kind, seeing such organizations as distracting the working class from the broader ideological issues. The national union organizations were, moreover, preoccupied with extending their power on another front through *interprofessional* agreements negotiated on a national level; several of these agreements were signed between 1968 and 1975 and gave the unions a central role in such critical institutions as the social security system. The unions could not afford to let plant-level developments among their constituencies escape their control, but they were not, on the other hand, unhappy to see it disintegrate.

The aftermath of 1968 thus left ample scope for a secondary sector to restore the flexibility which the reforms in the primary sector removed. That sector has been developed through three basic institutions: temporary help services, subcontracting, and plant decentralization.

For the role of subcontracting in this regard, there are no national figures, and we are forced to rely exclusively upon case studies and anecdotal evidence, which is abundant. Virtually every French investigator with field experience can recount one or another story about a major producer who monitors his demand and attempts to transfer an unsustainable increase to smaller, independent producers. The systematic studies which bear on this problem are the Annecy study of labor mobility, conducted by the *Centre d'étude de l'emploi*;[31] a study of the industrial and labor market structures of the Saint-Etienne region;[32] and a study of subcontracting in the French automobile industry.[33] The Annecy study, probably the most comprehensive local labor market study ever conducted, followed the labor movement from January 1968 through June 1969 and used both workers' job histories and personnel actions in a sample of employing units. The study identified two distinct classes of workers and of establishments: a class of stable workers and stable jobs, and a class of workers and jobs in which mobility was concentrated. A major component of the unstable jobs is found in enterprises of ten to one hundred employees who work as subcontractors and whose demand for labor is, as a consequence, extremely irregular. The findings of the Saint-Etienne and the automobile industry studies (which overlap) essentially parallel those of the Annecy study. The statistical work is less comprehensive, but a good deal more attention was paid to the precise relationship between the major producer and the subcontractor. The Saint-Etienne study is also noteworthy because of the distinction which it draws between the 1962–7 period and the 1968–73 period. The growth in dependent subcontracts is clearly a phenomenon of the second period.

The growth of temporary help services since 1968 is somewhat easier to document in statistical terms, though temporary help services were only brought under official control in 1973. The data before that time must be built up out of a variety of special surveys. The data do apparently support the conclusion that since 1955 "the number, activity and diversity of temporary help services has grown continually in France and the rate of expansion, marked even in 1955, accelerated perceptively from 1968 to 1972."[34] The value added by these enterprises tripled in the 1968 to 1972 period.[35] Over half of the enterprises in France drew on temporary workers in 1968; the figure is presumably much larger now.[36] Temporary help agencies were originally created to cover vacations and absences of permanent employees, particularly office workers. The shift toward the function of generating flexibility in labor utilization and avoiding permanent employment obligations is suggested by a survey of employers which shows that 50 percent utilize temporary help services to cover occasional peaks in activity and 11 percent for seasonal work; 37 percent of the temporary personnel are apparently production workers (as opposed to office workers, 34 percent, and sales help, 7 percent).[37] The largest single industrial user is heavy manufacturing, which tends to support the hypothesis that resorting to these agencies is a response of large enterprises to increased worker militancy in the shop and restrictions upon layoff and discharge.[38] A 1969 survey of permanent workers found that 65 percent believed temporary help services were being used to resolve "certain personnel problems" connected with the creation of permanent positions.[39] On this point, there is also ample anecdotal evidence from employers. A particularly dramatic – but not usual – case was a large international company which began employing temporary help in production in anticipation of a change in plant location two years hence. This company claimed that they felt such an approach was essential if they were to secure the approval of the *inspecteur du travail* when the time came.[40]

In addition to temporary help services, which in effect subcontract employment, a number of employers also hire temporary help on their own payrolls and manage in this way to avoid permanent employment obligations and the review of the *inspecteur du travail* in the case of layoffs. This practice of creating temporary positions is widespread in the public service. Magaud, who studied this phenomenon, found (his statistics stop in 1967) that three-quarters of state employees were permanent (*titulaire*) and the remaining 25 percent were temporary (*vacataire*). Magaud argues along lines very similar to our own that the situation in the public sector is typical of employment contracts, which the greater diversity of the private sector obscures. Various examples from the private sector substantiate this point but the kind of statistics which would enable us to trace the evolution of these arrangements over time are lacking.[41]

The French labor market structure cannot be described in terms of institutions alone. The duality which emerged after 1968 appears also to be dependent upon the identification and deployment of labor force groups which are either indifferent to the flux and uncertainty of the secondary sector or lack the political power and social cohesion to resist the economic functions which that sector has been called upon to support. Special groups of this kind are particularly necessary, given the fact that the institutional structure which emerged in 1968 did not create a sharp distinction between labor market spheres. Rather, its effect was to increase the *sensitivity* of the system to differentials in workers' resistance or acquiescence to employers' efforts to use them as the residual adjustment factor in the production process. Four types of workers have formed the "acquiescent" portion of the labor force, which has made the secondary sector viable: youth, women, migrants, and peasants.

The direct evidence that these particular groups are being used in this way is largely anecdotal with a certain amount of statistical evidence to this effect in the case of temporary help services. The study of the Compiègne labor market by the *Centre d'étude de l'emploi* has made a special effort to concentrate on this question, and preliminary results show that temporary help is more concentrated among women and immigrants than is permanent help in an enterprise by enterprise comparison. Another study of temporary workers notes a concentration among women, youth, single, and married without children relative to the proportion of these groups in the labor force at large. There is considerable indirect evidence in the way in which the character of economic expansion and its impact upon the structure of employment and unemployment shifted after 1968. The following points are notable in this regard:

First, the immediate effect of the *accords de Grenelle* was to set off a rapid economic expansion fueled by the wage increases embodied in the agreement. The expansion was in marked contrast to the preceding period. The composition of unemployment shifted away from a relative concentration among women and youth and toward older workers.[42] There was also an increased reliance in 1969 upon immigration. Immigration, moreover, did not recede when the pace of the expansion slowed in 1970 as it had in similar periods in the past.[43] Thus, overall, the immediate post-1968 expansion appears to have been one in which employers turned away from older, less flexible workers toward the more pliable labor force groups.

Second, there has been an unusual increase in the labor force participation of adult women. The rate of female labor force participation, which had been fairly constant since the beginning of the century, suddenly increased in the 1962–8 period and further accelerated after 1968. The rate which was 40 percent in 1962 reached 45 percent in 1968, 47 percent in 1970, and 52 percent in 1975. Of special interest in the present context is the apparent displacement of men in unskilled and semiskilled industrial jobs. Thus, for example, in the machinery industry women constituted 21 percent of the labor force in 1968 but 39 percent of the employment increase between 1968 and 1973; in other industries the comparable figures are 18 and 61 percent, respectively. The trend is also evident in occupational statistics: the number of men in unskilled and semiskilled jobs (*manoeuvres and ouvriers specialisés*) declined 18 and 5 percent, respectively, between 1968 and 1973; the number of women increased by 10 percent and 14 percent.[44]

Third, the increase in female employment was accompanied by an increase in female unemployment. The two seem to be causally related: unemployment has increased in the regions where employment is also rising. The rising unemployment, moreover, is concentrated among experienced female workers and cannot, therefore, be attributed to the search of new entrants for jobs. This is consistent with our notion that in the post-1968 period employers actively sought out new female workers because they could be made to bear the flux and uncertainity to which the customary labor force was becoming increasingly resistant. The female labor force participation rates rose in response to these active recruitment efforts, but since the new workers were being drawn directly into employment, they did not show up in unemployment rates. The unemployment rates for experienced workers rose, however, as the contingencies for which the new workers were being recruited began to occur, and they were laid off or, in anticipation of such a layoff, quit to look for another job.[45] There is a parallel increase in the unemployment of youth, also concentrated among experienced youth workers, and suggesting that they, like women, are increasingly bearing the flux and uncertainty of economic activity.[46] Although it is somewhat premature to draw definitive lessons from the current economic recession, it appears that a second jump in the structural component of female and youth unemployment occurred in 1975 in response to the new restrictions upon layoff and discharge.[47]

Fourth, the pattern of utilization of immigrant labor has shifted in ways which parallel the shifts in female employment. It is difficult to estimate the number of foreign workers in France, but it appears that the rate of increase was not markedly different in the 1968–74 period from that of the 1962–8 period. The response of immigration to the business cycle did change, however. Prior to 1968, the foreign labor force had varied systematically with economic activity. After 1968, this labor force was a lot less responsive to these variations. As already noted, it continued, in fact, to grow after 1970 when overall employment slowed and unemployment increased. Only after the 1974 recession was a serious effort made to reduce the foreign labor force. That effort involved a major campaign to induce them to return home and special institutional restrictions upon reentry and work in France.[48]

Finally, the most striking piece of evidence in support of this overall thesis was the shift in the index of *marge de production sans embauche*. This may be roughly translated as the "margin of output available without new hires." The index is based upon a questionnaire administered to employers and is roughly speaking, a measure of the excess labor capacity maintained to absorb variations in demand. After 1960, the index "which had remained relatively stable around ten percent began to decline and subsequently stabilized again around six percent." The decline suggests that after 1968 employers relied less upon internal labor reserves and more upon the external labor market.[49]

The United States

The contemporary United States labor market is embedded in an institutional structure which derives from the Great Depression of the 1930s and the reforms of the "second" New Deal. These include the National Labor Relations Act, which defined the role and scope of trade union activity, the Social Security Act, which introduced both old-age pensions and unemployment insurance, and the Fair Labor Standards Act, which established the minimum wage and other minimal labor standards. The critical historical events, however, were not these reforms themselves but the massive waves of labor protest of 1936 and 1937 which postdate the institutional changes.

The 1936–7 period in the United States is remarkably similar to May 1968 in France and 1969 and its aftermath in Italy.[50] The similarities extend from the specific tactics of the rank and file workers to the ultimate effects upon the structure of the labor market and includes the general climate which the labor unrest generated in the society at large and among established trade union and managerial leaders in particular. The period was characterized by sudden unanticipated labor unrest, expressing itself in a wave of wildcat sit-down strikes and the spontaneous development of work-place level organization throughout the mass production industries, which had previously been resistant to union organization. The sit-downs began in the rubber industry in January 1936 and spread to autos, steel, textiles, oil refining, and ship building. The most dramatic strikes were in the automobile industry, where on New Year's Eve of 1936 a few hundred workers seized General Motors plants in Flint, Michigan, precipitating a strike which lasted forty-five days, eventually involved 44,000 workers, and culminated in the company's recognition of the union.

The strikes and the organizations which grew out of them were profoundly disturbing to established union leaders. The sit-down tactic, involving as it did the occupation of private property, was unconventional, clearly illegal, and anathema to the professed ideology of the American labor movement. The organizations which emerged through the strikes were industrial unions grouping in a single local all the workers in a plant and, in this way, violating the traditional craft lines along which the American labor movement was then organized. The new tactics and organizational forms became the fulcrum around which the conflict between older and younger labor leaders developed and by 1938 produced the split between the old AFL and the CIO, which was built around and incorporated the movement that arose during the period. The impact upon the employers was generally profound, and led to a general reappraisal of their traditional overt hostility toward labor organization. That change in attitude was officially signaled by the voluntary capitulation of United States Steel to the CIO Steel Workers Organizing Committee without a strike in the spring of 1937. The overall impact of this period is described by one author, in an otherwise rather dry textbook, in passages that might have been lifted from a French account of 1968:

The workers themselves sensed possession of a new economic and political power. The result was a virtual uprising of worker protest across the nation, reaching its peak about 1937 with a militancy that bred in defenders of the established order a fear that the society which they knew and prized was breaking open around them. . . . It is difficult for one who did not live through this period to appreciate its electrical quality. The writer of this book was in 1937 a reporter – he can recall very vividly visiting the winter before a friend who was a reporter in the Akron area and with him touring the [occupied] plants of the Goodyear Rubber Company. . . . These were times when one sensed that a new society was stirring in the womb of the old.[51]

The institutional arrangements. Because of the depressed economic conditions in which the expanded labor movement developed,
employment security was a central bargaining issue. Indeed, after the
recognition and security of the union itself, it was probably the single
most important concern of the newly organized unions. That concern
was met through a series of provisions in locally negotiated agreements at the plant or work-place level that governed economic layoff,
promotion and disciplinary discharge.[52]

Several points should be made about the impact of these arrangements upon job security and, more broadly, upon the employer's
ability to deploy labor at will. First, employers in the United States
never conceded the absolute right to job security which arose in
France and Italy in the 1960s. Instead, unions negotiated a series of
seniority arrangements in which the employer retained the right to
reduce the level of employment at his discretion, in response to variations in business conditions. But he was obligated to do so in accord
with rules negotiated with trade unions. Generally, these rules gave
very heavy weight to seniority, creating a system in which the last
hired was the first fired. The employer was obligated to rehire in order
of layoff. In the eyes of class-conscious European unionism, what was
involved in this arrangement was a hollow settlement in which the
issue of the distribution of insecurity between labor and management
was compromised in favor of arrangements which simply distributed
insecurity among members of the labor force. There is a certain
amount of truth in this proposition. Indeed, the attraction of seniority
can probably only be understood in distributional terms: it removes,
once and for all, the responsibility from union leaders of distributing
among their constituents the employment insecurity which they cannot eliminate and, for the workers, it is the one foolproof distributional criterion in a situation which otherwise lends itself to fa-
voritism, abuse, and corruption. However, these arrangements, *in
fact*, do act as a barrier to layoffs, thus enhancing the security of all
employees. Because they do so, they also create incentives to restore
flexibility similar in kind, although probably less severe, to those inherent in the European system. The barriers to layoffs come from the
fact that the employer cannot pick and choose among his work force
and is obliged frequently to lay off the more productive employees. Of
equal importance in this regard is a feature of the typical American
system which links the rules governing layoffs to a system of internal
job distribution. The result of this is that every layoff typically involves a considerable redistribution of the remaining jobs in the estab-
lishment. The movement involved in that redistribution is expensive,

and the expense is compounded by the fact that the employer has very little control over who gets distributed where.

This is related to another critical feature of the system instituted by union organizations in the 1930s: The job security arrangements in American industry are only meaningful if the jobs are very carefully defined and their content continually monitored. Any change in job content and in the redistribution of tasks will involve changes in the effective job security of the employees. As a result, the union has an intimate interest in job definition and carefully monitors not only technological changes but also shifts in job content which result from day to day shifts in production levels and in the composition of output.[53] While "technology" in the United States nominally remains a managerial prerogative, and the ideology would seem to give employers a good deal more freedom in this regard than in, for example, Italy, American management has in fact faced similar inhibitions throughout the postwar period.

Finally, what is true with respect to technological change is also true with respect to discipline. American unions have never challenged management's right to discipline workers for "cause" but they have insisted that the "cause" be understood in advance and that the discipline be administered in accord with prenegotiated standards of due process. American management believed when these new standards were first introduced in the 1930s that they seriously weakened disciplinary control. The ideology of American industrial relations seems to leave management with more control than in Italy but the advent of unions was perceived by American management in the postwar period much as it was perceived by Italian management after 1969.

The net result of the emergence of industrial unions in the 1930s was thus a system which, from a managerial point of view, was a good deal more rigid. In contrast to the post-1968 systems of France and Italy, it is probably less inflexible with respect to the level of employment but more so with respect to the degree to which labor can be assigned in a discretionary and supple way.

The full impact of these changes did not emerge immediately: their impact was delayed and, in the final analysis, probably aggravated by World War II. It was not clear at the time whether the union gains in 1936 and 1937 were permanent or merely a tactical retreat on the part of employers. American labor history prior to 1936 can be read as a seesaw battle between labor and capital in which management periodically retreated in the face of strong worker resistance, biding its time until the economic and political climate turned in its favor and then reversing its policy in order to break the union. The concessions of 1936 and 1937 could be seen as merely another such episode in this battle, and it is probable that the important managerial figures in steel and autos did indeed anticipate a reversal in a more favorable political climate once the anger and frustration of the rank and file had been spent. Several factors, however, intervened to solidify labor's position and forestall any effort by management to reduce union gains. Among these was the labor legislation, passed before the sit-down strikes, but only endorsed by the Supreme Court in 1938, which legitimized union organization and collective bargaining. Because the Court had been so hostile to earlier New Deal reforms, and had actually struck down the National Industrial Recovery Act which embodied many of the features of the new legislation, its approval was at least as important as the passage of the legislation itself, and, indeed, after the concessions of big steel, the rest of that industry held out against the unions until the Court had acted.

The second facilitating factor was the change in the organizational structure and ideology of the American labor movement. After the organization of autos and big steel, the CIO became a permanent, powerful organizational entity and the old AFL quickly reversed its historic position and began to charter and organize industrial unions as well. In the process, the labor movement not only consolidated the spontaneous rank-and-file movement into permanent organizational entities; it also acquired enormous financial resources from its new membership base which enabled it to undertake further organizational drives and to create a credible threat of resistance to employer counterattacks.

But the third, and possibly critical, factor was the war itself. The exigencies of wartime production forced management and organized labor to work closely together in a way which implied mutual acceptance. The effect was undoubtedly to reenforce the American tradition of business unionism with its underlying acceptance of and respect for the prevailing economic system among the new, and originally more radical, generation of trade union leaders.[54] But the war also bred a new generation of management, who cultivated an ability to work with the new unions and had, in fact, built their careers upon the new institutional structure. They genuinely accepted union organization. Without the war, this same generation of managers might have been engaged in planning and implementing the kind of counterattack which had undermined the union gains of earlier periods in American history.

Along with the basic acceptance of the strength and permanence of the new worker organizations, however, industrial managers came to resent deeply the limitations which union work rules placed upon their operational freedom. The postwar resentment was the product of two factors. First, the impact of wartime conditions was, essentially, to suspend the operation of the layoffs rules; given the pressures of war demand, production virtually never declined and in those rare instances when it did, layoffs were deterred by the tight labor market and the consequent difficulties of replacing lost labor. Thus, the first real operating experience under the new union restrictions came after the war. Second, the conditions of wartime production had themselves resulted in practices which made union rules particularly onerous. Under wartime pressures, employers had hired virtually any "warm body"; the seniority system committed them in the postwar period not only to the continued employment of these "bodies" but to certain patterns of promotion as well. The nature of union grievance procedures added an additional set of problems. Those procedures place tremendous weight upon past practice in defining what was legitimate in routine shop discipline. As a result, lax procedures, which had grown up during the war when acute production pressures, combined with tight labor markets which discourage discharge, were carried over into the postwar period. The result is that, despite the distinctive institutional structure of the United States and the apparently greater flexibility in the utilization of labor which it allows, the complaints of American management in the immediate postwar were very similar to those voiced currently in France and Italy with respect to layoffs and discipline. The result of this set of managerial attitudes was a concerted effort to restore the flexibility which the seniority system combined with wartime operating procedures had removed.

The efforts themselves may be classed under three headings. First, there was an attempt to loosen up restrictive practice through persuasion in labor negotiations and a tougher line in bargaining. As we have noted, the system of layoffs and the focus upon process as opposed to substance in discipline makes the United States system potentially a good deal less restrictive than the European, and management made a concerted effort in the postwar period to realize that potential. It is difficult to say how successful these efforts were but obviously, to the extent that they succeeded, they avoided the kind of dichotomy in the labor market upon which this chapter has focused.

Second, as we have also noted, a number of managements sought to avoid the restrictions upon job definition and labor utilization which the seniority system entailed by guaranteeing employment. Some of those efforts were part of a nonunion strategy. Others were negotiated with trade unions, usually as part of a package which smoothed the way for major technological changes. The basic impact of such efforts is to generate a dichotomous labor market structure, precisely analogous to that in Italy or France. When these arrangements were negotiated with the union, they often introduced the dichotomy into the work place itself. This arrangement is standard in the sugar refining industry; employees hired before 1957 and guaranteed jobs work side by side with later hires who have no guarantees at all. It is also the case for dock workers. Nonunion manufacturing employees appear to rely on subcontracting: managers are continually operating on the margin of what is known as the make-buy decision. They only expand their own payrolls if the increase in production in-house appears sustainable over the long run; and, in the short run, there is a corresponding effort to reduce subcontracting and increase the percentage of output produced in-house in periods of slack production.

The third employer response had been a tendency to maximize the degree of flexibility within the current structure of rules. This involves a series of different strategies, all of which tend to enhance the dichotomous structure of the labor market. Among these strategies are an effort to avoid permanent hiring in tight labor markets where the seniority system would freeze into the employment structure substandard employees. The institutions utilized to avoid permanent hires are temporary help services, subcontracting, and recycling of employees through a probationary period, discharging new workers before they acquire union membership rights and permanent employment status. Another strategy has been to seek to evade the legislation altogether through plant locations in nonunion areas, largely the rural Midwest and South and through reliance upon groups of workers with a high turnover and a low propensity to join the union such as women, youths, and blacks. In some industries, it appears that the unions themselves have countenanced a certain amount of such shifting by entering into tacit agreements with employers to permit more flexible work arrangements in some shops in return for assurances that this form of subcontracting will be limited and that the shops will meet union scales. Again, this is easiest when the labor force is such that shops are composed of relatively weak, docile, and high-turnover groups. Indeed, we can view these arrangements as an almost inevitable development in certain industries. It would take an extraordinary effort of education and indoctrination on the part of the union, for example, to raise the consciousness of the work force in small garment shops to that maintained in the largest productive units.

Statistical documentation of these institutional patterns are unavailable. (My own understanding of these patterns developed in the middle sixties while studying seniority structures in manufacturing at the same time that I was concerned with employment complaints from black ghetto workers.[55]) Evidence for the existence of the attitudes and institutional patterns can be found in the seniority and grievance procedures which dominate the personnel literature in the immediate postwar period. The resurgence of union concern with job security in the late 1950s, during the so-called automation crisis, generated a literature about subcontracting and its relations to seniority arrangements and employment guarantees. The volume of pamphlet material, the prominence accorded the issues in public policy discussions and in professional managerial literature, and the variety of different industries affected all suggest the importance of the issues at stake, although they do not permit any quantitative estimates.

As the foregoing suggests, these arrangements which introduce flexibility into the United States industrial relations system also depend heavily upon certain divisions of the labor force, in particular, upon women, youth, minorities (especially blacks), rural workers, and lately foreign laborers, all of whom are either more willing to act as a "residual" factor of production or less able to resist. The postwar period has seen a decline of prime "adult" male labor force relative to all other groups.

It is, of course, impossible to separate from the statistics the effects of employer actions, especially those motivated by the desire to enhance work force flexibility, from autonomous changes in labor supply. Certain of the changes in employment patterns, however, have been quite clearly an effort to restore flexibility. Employers have spoken relatively openly throughout the postwar period about the movement out of urban industrial centers in terms of union constraints. This is especially clear in the case of the South, which has actively appealed to employers on this basis; but it is also mentioned, albeit more circumspectly, in the case of moves to the rural Midwest. Interviews with employers who have recently been hiring foreign workers in large numbers reveal that these workers are replacing the black labor force which, since the middle sixties, has become militantly resistant to work which lacks the job security and procedural guarantees available to the white labor force.[56] These interviews not only quite clearly indicate the current role of foreign workers in the United States labor market but also suggest the role black workers played in Northern urban labor markets in previous decades. A tendency to have used the blacks to inhibit the rigidification of the labor force, first by the threat of and if need be the actual substitution of blacks for other workers, is also evident in the histories of particular unions and industries.

The postwar baby boom, the expansion of education and the part-time student workers it produced, and the increased labor force participation of women were trends that could be used to provide flexibility. The particular way in which our educational system has expanded, by extending the period in school into adulthood rather than by pushing it back toward infancy, has served to reduce the permanent, full-time labor force among *both* women and youth and in this way contributed to the development of a flexible supply of labor. Even apparently autonomous trends in labor supply can thus be seen as importantly influenced by public policy in ways unlikely to lie completely beyond the politics of labor market structure.

The theoretical implications of historical experience

The similarities in the developments in all three countries shed some light on the questions suggested earlier about the underlying causes of duality. First, in all three cases, the expansion if not the actual development of the secondary sector occurred in response to a sudden upsurge of labor militancy. This leads us to be very skeptical of theories which suggest that the real cause of rigidification is investment in human capital, however important this may be in the microeconomic dualism of particular industries. The nature of that militancy also leads us to suspect theories of implicit contract. Such theories are most plausible in the United States, where the militancy arose in the midst of the Depression and could be interpreted as the outgrowth of the changes in attitudes toward flux and uncertainty which the Depression generated. However, even in the United States, the nature of the worker revolt belies the concept of "rationality" upon which theories of implicit contract are built; of course, in France and Italy, there is not even a depression to account for the sudden change in worker attitudes which the implicit contract theory would require.

Next, again in all three cases, the institutional arrangements through which the distinction between the primary and secondary sectors is effectuated appear to be "found" rather than "made." In the United States, those arrangements grew up within a framework of labor and social security legislation passed in the early 1930s, whereas the labor militancy was a product of the late 1930s and its realization in labor organization of the 1940s. The various exemptions, de facto and de jure, in the labor legislation which made room for the secondary sector, seemed to be the product of the Roosevelt electoral coalition, which married urban-industrial working class with old-line Southern power structure and a small business class, which in other nations would be called the petty bourgeoisie. In Italy, the secondary institutions seem also to predate the use to which they were put and to be an attempt to protect certain traditional classes of small business. Thus we tend to be very skeptical of conspiratorial explanations, at least in so far as they focus upon the nature of the institutional structure. The causes of the process seem to lie within the nature of the capitalist system, but it is less clear that the institutional response is a deliberate attempt to respond to that pressure.

The third similarity in all these countries is that the labor force for secondary jobs tends to rely heavily, although not exclusively, upon preindustrial groups and classes. In part, it is the existence of these classes which make the institutions work in favor of the secondary sector. In the case of migrants (both domestic and foreign), for example, employers have been very active in recruitment, and it is very doubtful that the migration process would have reached this volume without the employer initiative. Similarly, female unemployment rates in rural France, which show a paradoxical tendency to *rise* with industrial employment, seem to reflect an employment policy designed to draw forth a secondary labor force.

On the other hand, the capitalist system *finds* these classes and *does not create* them. Even in the case of the women in rural France, it appears that the unemployment rates are less a reflection of a *change* in attitude produced by the appearance of industrial jobs than an *expression* of attitudes, which in the absence of employment opportunities remained latent. The migrants (foreign and domestic), the rural workers, and the women are attractive precisely because they belong to another socioeconomic structure and view industrial employment as a temporary adjunct to their primary roles. They are willing to take temporary jobs because they see their commitment to these jobs as temporary, and they are able to bear the flux and uncertainty of the industrial economy because they have traditional economic activities upon which to fall back.

NOTES

1. I am indebted to Guy Roustang for this point. It derives from his study in Françoise Guélaud et al., *Pour une analyse des conditions du travail ouvrier dans l'entreprise* (Paris: Librairie Armand Colin, 1975). See also: Michael J. Piore, "The Impact of the Labor Market on the Design and Selection of Productive Techniques within the Manufacturing Plant," *Quarterly Journal of Economics, 82* (November 1968), no. 4, 602–20.
2. Walter Oi, "Labor as a Quasi-Fixed Factor," *The Journal of Political Economy, 70* (December 1962), no. 6, 538–55. Also, Gary Becker, *Human Capital* (New York: Columbia University Press, 1969).

3. Marcia Freedman, *Labor Markets: Segments and Shelters* (Montclair, N.J.: Allenhold, Osmun, 1976). Also along these lines, see Michael J. Piore, "Upward Mobility, Job Monotony and Labor Market Structure," in James O'Toole (ed.), *Work and the Quality of Life* (Cambridge, Mass.: MIT Press, 1974), pp. 73–87.
4. For example, C. Azariadis, "Implicit Contracts and Underdevelopment Equilibrium," *Journal of Political Economy* (August 1975).
5. Stephen A. Marglin, "What Do Bosses Do? The Origins and Functions of Hierarchy in Capitalist Production," and Katherine Stone, "The Origins of Job Structures in the Steel Industry," *The Review of Radical Political Economy*, 6 (Summer 1974), no. 2, 60–173.
6. Roger Cornu, *Mineurs cévenols et provençaux face à la crise des charbonnages* (Aix-en-Provence: Laboratoire d'économie et de sociologie du travail, May 1975), Ch. 1, pp. 24–55.
7. Lisa Peattie, "The Other Sector: A Few Facts from Bogotá, Some Comments and a List of Issues" (mimeo., June 1974).
8. David Brody, *The Steel Workers in America: The Non-Union Era* (Cambridge, Mass.: Harvard University Press, 1960).
9. Many of these studies are reported in Massimo Paci, *Mercato del lavoro e classi sociali in Italia* (Bologna: Il Mulino, 1973). See also Berger, Chapter 4 of this present book, and Suzanne Berger, "The Uses of the Traditional Sector: Why the Declining Classes Survive," in F. Bechhofer and B. Elliott, *The Petty Bourgeoisie* (London: Macmillan, 1980).
10. Michel Destefanis and Anne-Marie Vasseur, *Le Fonctionnement d'un marché du travail local* (Paris: Cahiers du centre d'études de l'emploi, Presses Universitaires de France, 1974).
11. Robert Berrier, *The Politics of Industrial Survival, The French Textile Industry*, unpublished doctoral dissertation; Massachusetts Institute of Technology, 1978.
12. Jacques Magaud, "Vrais et faux salariés," *Sociologie du travail* (January–March 1974), no. 1, 1–18.
13. The section on Italy draws heavily upon Berger's research reported in this volume and on two English language reviews of the Italian literature. One was written as part of this project by Judith Chubb, "The Functions of Economic 'Marginality': The Case of Italy," M.I.T. Political Science Dept., mimeo., September 1975; the other, focusing more broadly upon industrial relations research, by Gino Giugni, "Industrial Relations Research in Italy," paper prepared for a conference on Industrial Relations Research in Contemporary Industrial Society, Harvard University, September 1975.
14. The clearest example among all industrialized countries is, of course, Japan, but the discussion of that case is for our purposes confused by the question of how much the origins of dualism have to do with the particular characteristics of Japanese culture. See, for example, Ronald Dore, *British Factory, Japanese Factory: The Origins of National Diversity in*

Industrial Relations (Berkeley: University of California Press, 1973); Robert Evans, *The Labor Economies of Japan and the United States* (New York: Praeger, 1971).

15. See for example, George J. Hildebrand, *Growth and Structure in the Economy of Modern Italy* (Cambridge, Mass.: Harvard University Press, 1965), pp. 272–301; and Vera Lutz, *Italy, A Study in Economic Development* (London: Oxford University Press, 1962).

16. For an interpretation of the Italian experience which stresses the historical importance of shop-level organization, see B. Salvati, "The Rebirth of Italian Trade Unionism, 1943–54," in S. J. Woolf (ed.), *The Rebirth of Italy, 1943–50* (London: Longman, 1972), pp. 181–211; Giugni, "Industrial Relations Research," also uses several studies which support this point.

17. Salvati, *Rebirth of Italy*.

18. See Federico Butera, "Mutamento dell'organizzazione del lavoro ed egemonia," *Economia e Lavoro* (January–February 1976), no. 1, 39–80.

19. This view is summarized in Libero Lenti, *Grandeur et servitudes de l'économie italienne* (Paris: Calmann-Levy, 1973), esp. pp. 268–74.

20. Massimo Paci, *Mercato del lavoro e classi sociali in Italia* (Bologna: Il Mulino, 1973), pp. 322–30.

21. *Ibid.*, pp. 330–4.

22. See Chapter 4 here and also Berger's "The Uses of the Traditional Sector" in Bechhofer and Elliott.

23. Massimo Paci, "The 'Dual' Labor Market as a Strategy of Italian Industry," prepared for the Organisation for Economic Cooperation and Development, mimeo., 1975, p. 8.

24. See Chapter 4.

25. Berger, Chapter 4, pp. 20–1; also "Il lavoro a domicilio," a special issue of *Quaderni di Rassegna sindacale*, 11 (September–December 1973) no. 44–5; and Luigi Frey (ed.), *Lavoro a domicilio e decentramento dell' attività produttiva nei settori tessile e dell' abbigliamento in Italia* (Milan: F. Angeli, 1975).

26. Paci (1973), *Mercato del lavoro e classi sociali*.

27. This and the subsequent discussion are based upon Francis Naude et Aude Benoit, "Licenciements collectifs et securité de l'emploi," *Droit social* (June 1975), no. 6, 41–52; Jean Pierre Duprilot, "Le contrôle administratif des licenciements," *Droit social* (June 1975), no. 6, 53–72; and Frederic Meyers, *Ownership of Jobs: A Comparative Study* (Los Angeles: University of California Press, 1964), pp. 44–73. On the impact of these changes on employers, see Suzanne Berger, "Lame Ducks and National Champions: French Industrial Policy in the Fifth Republic," in W. Andrews and S. Hoffmann, *The Fifth Republic at Twenty* (Brockport: State University of New York Press, 1980).

28. See "Le Comité d'entreprise et la section syndicale," *Les Cahiers français*,

notice 4 (Mai–Août 1972), nos. 154–5; "Les Conventions collectives," *Les Cahiers français*, notice 3 (Mai–Août 1972), nos. 154–5; Gérard Adam et Michel Lucas, "Les Institutions de représentation du personnel en France: bilan et perspective," *Droit social* (Mars 1976), no. 3, 79–91; Dominique Martin, "Les Systems de négotiation et de représentation dans l'entreprise," *Droit social* (Mars 1976), no. 3, 92–101.

29. In 1975, for example, 35 percent of enterprises of 50 to 149 employees had a *section syndicale* compared to 62 percent in the 150 to 299 employee category and 96 percent in the over 1,000 category, *Travail international* (March 1976), no. 9, 22–8.

30. This point was apparent in my own limited interviews in France, but it was also made by the team of researchers working on the Annecy and Compiègne studies of the *Centre d'étude d'emploi*.

31. Michel Destefanis et Anne-Marie Vasseur, *Le Fonctionnement d'un marché du travail local, le bassin de main-d'oeuvre d'Annecy* (Presses Universitaires de France: Paris, 1974), pp. 158–60.

32. Centre de recherches et d'études sociologiques appliquées de la Loire [CRESAL], "L'Industrie à Saint-Etienne, caractéristiques et évolution dans l'aire du S.D.A.U. depuis 1962. Rapport de synthèse" (Mai 1975).

33. CRESAL, "Pratique et signification de la soustraitance dans l'industrie automobile en France," rapport au Comité d'organisation des recherches appliquées sur le développement économique et social [CORDES] (Mai 1973).

34. "Le Travail temporaire," *Les Cahiers français*, notice 2 (Novembre–Décembre 1975), no. 173, 1.

35. *Ibid.*

36. "Le Travail intérimaire en France," *Problèmes économiques* (10 Juin 1971), no. 1223, 22–6.

37. *Les Cahiers français*, notice 2, no. 173, "Le Travail temporaire," p. 2.

38. *Ibid.*

39. *Ibid.*, p. 4.

40. This story was related to me by one of the investigators at the *Centre d'étude de l'emploi*.

41. Magaud, "Vrais et faux salariés."

42. Robert Salais, "L'Emploi industriel a de nouveau augmenté de 1968 à 1969," *Economie et statistique* (Décembre 1969), no. 7, 20–1.

43. Bruno Durieux, "L'Evolution de l'emploi en 1970," *Economie et statistique* (Avril 1971), no. 22, 21.

44. François Eymard-Duvernay, "L'Emploi au cours du Vième plan," *Economie et statistique* (Janvier 1976), no. 74, 40–2. See also Catherine Giradeau, "Les Perspectives d'emploi d'ici à 1980," *Economie et statistique* (Juillet–Août 1975), no. 69, 38.

45. François Eymard-Duvernay et Robert Salais, "Une analyse des liens entre

l'emploi et le chômage," *Economie et statistique* (Juillet–Août 1975), no. 69, 23. Also see Claude Thélot, "Le Fonctionnement de marché de l'emploi: l'example des pays de la Loire," *Economie et statistique* (Juillet–Août 1975), no. 69, 51–8.

46. Pierre Mormiche, "Les Jeunes sur le marché de travail," *Economie et statistique* (Juillet–Août 1975), no. 69, 65–71.

47. Eymard-Duvernay (1976), "L'Emploi au cours du VIème plan," pp. 37–45.

48. *Ibid.*, p. 44. Also, Durieux (1971), "L'Evolution de l'emploi," and M. J. F. Girme, "France," in *Trends in the Use of External Sources of Labour in France, Germany, and Great Britain*, Bundesanstalt für Arbeit der Prasident, Nurnberg (December 1974).

49. Eymard-Duvernay (1976), "L'Emploi au cours du Vième plan," p. 43.

50. For the historical account which follows see, Walter Galenson, *The CIO Challenge to the AFL: A History of the American Labor Movement 1935–1941* (Cambridge, Mass.: Harvard University Press, 1960); Sidney Lens, *The Labor Wars: From the Molly Maguires to the Sit-Downs* (Garden City: Doubleday, 1973); and Philip Taft, *Organized Labor in American History* (New York: Harper & Row, 1964).

51. Niel W. Chamberlain, *The Labor Sector* (New York: McGraw-Hill, 1965), p. 127.

52. For a detailed description of industrial relations institutions at the plant level in the United States, see Peter B. Doeringer and Michael J. Piore, *Internal Labor Markets and Manpower Analyses* (Lexington, Mass.: D. C. Heath, 1971), esp. pp. 1–132; and Sumner Slichter, James J. Healy, and E. Robert Livernash, *The Impact of Collective Bargaining on Management* (Washington: The Brookings Institution, 1960).

53. Michael J. Piore, "Job Monotony, Employment Security and Upward Mobility in the Labor Market," in Louis E. Davis and Albert B. Cherns (eds.), *The Quality of Working Life*, Vol. I (New York: The Free Press, 1975), pp. 354–6.

54. One must add in this regard, however, the role of the postwar purge of communist labor leaders, which insured that those who were ideologically resistant to the cooperative forms of labor-management relations that developed during the war were removed.

55. Michael J. Piore, "On the Job Training in a Dual Labor Market," in Arnold Weber et al., *Public-Private Manpower Policies* (Madison, Wis.: Industrial Relations Research Association, 1969), pp. 101–32.

56. Michael J. Piore, "Immigration, Work Experience, and Labor Market Structure," in Pastora San Juan Cafferty and Leon Chestang (eds.), *The Diverse Society* (Washington, D.C.: National Association of Social Workers, 1976), pp. 109–28.

3

THE TECHNOLOGICAL
FOUNDATIONS OF DUALISM
AND DISCONTINUITY

This chapter develops a view of discontinuities in economic structure as the outgrowth of the evolution of technology in the course of economic development. It is directed particularly at the relationship between the structure of the labor market and other discontinuities in the economic structure which have been associated with labor market structure in the literature and which, like the structure of the labor market, are often characterized as dualistic. The argument here is meant to be complementary to the view presented in the preceding chapter, where dualism in the dual labor market was seen as the outgrowth of a particular episode in the historical evolution of labor-management relations. It focuses upon the basic technical relationships which underlie industrial society, sets the limits upon the range of actual historical experience which occurs within it, and determines the points at which discontinuities are possible and likely to arise.

Discontinuities in the economic structure

The types of discontinuities which this chapter attempts to relate are threefold: (1) a dichotomy in the structure of enterprises of modern industrial economies between large, monopolistic or oligopolistic firms and a fringe or periphery of small, competitive enterprises; (2) a dichotomy in underdeveloped, or developing, economies between one sector, often characterized as modern or organized, and a second, traditional or informal sector; and (3) the stratified structure of the labor market, composed of a secondary and a primary sector, with further divisions in the latter separating professional and managerial positions from stable, blue collar jobs.

Each of these distinctions defines a typology of enterprises or workers based on differences among the behavioral patterns of the various "types." As noted above, it is such differences in behavior patterns which constitute the challenge posed by these typologies to conventional economic theory, for the latter postulates a single behavioral pattern of a kind that can be said to characterize the behavior of at best but one of the types identified in the typologies under consideration here. These different structures also affect the distribution of economic welfare of populations within the system as that welfare is mediated through such variables as income, security, status, or prestige. The typology of the labor market structure with which we will be concerned was discussed in the introductory section. It is necessary, however, to review the two other typologies, which we are attempting to relate in somewhat more detail before proceeding.

The structure of enterprises in developed economies

The notion of dualism in the structure of enterprises of developed economies was originally put forward by Robert Averitt in his book *The Dual Economy;*[1] it also emerged, apparently coincidentally, in the debate provoked by the publication, first of Robin Marris's *The Economics of Managerial Capitalism*[2] and then Galbraith's *The New Industrial State.*[3] Both Marris and Galbraith attacked the conventional notion of the competitive firm and asserted a view in which business enterprises in modern industrial society were depicted as large oligopolistic or monopolistic firms preoccupied with growth and market share, independently of and sometimes at the cost of profit maximization, and operating in markets which they planned and controlled themselves. These large firms control not only the price and quantity of their output but also the stability and uncertainty of demand and, through large reserves of internal funds, the capital required for production.

Averitt argues that such firms are only one sector of a dual economy. He terms that sector the *center*. The other sector, which Averitt terms the *periphery*, is composed of smaller, competitive enterprises. In this second sector fall most of the examples which the orthodox critics of Marris and Galbraith cite in defense of conventional theory.[4] These firms are relatively small; they are so tightly constrained by the market that it determines their decisions about price, quantity, and capital investments. They are basically motivated by a desire to survive and earn a profit and have no independent interest in growth or in a share of the market, which in any case they are powerless to affect and unable to perceive as a whole.

Dualism in underdeveloped economies

The second notion of dualism is found in the literature on underdeveloped countries.[5] It concentrates on the differences between an undeveloped sector and a modern one, which is often composed of very large firms using up-to-date technologies that generally originate in industrialized nations, are highly capital intensive, and require skilled technical manpower. These large firms tend to be foreign owned, or controlled, and export oriented. They coexist with traditional small-scale enterprises catering to the local market. The early literature tended to focus on peasant agriculture as the exemplar of these small-scale firms, but more recent work (for example, that of Peattie, who collaborated on the original project for this volume) focuses upon small-scale manufacturing and commerce in large urban areas.[6] While there is a tendency in the literature to associate these small-scale operations with low income, unorganized markets, Peattie's work makes clear that this may be quite misleading. Some of the markets are highly organized and appear to generate relatively high incomes for the people who run the enterprises, if not for their employees. If we include among the small-scale enterprises independent professionals such as doctors, lawyers, and local money lenders, who share many of the characteristics of other small firms, even the social status of people engaged in this other sector may be relatively high. The literature has usually assumed that these industries are the vestiges of a preindustrial economy which shrinks as development proceeds and ultimately disappears. But this notion is refuted in the two chapters by Suzanne Berger on the advanced economies of France and Italy in this volume, as well as by the discovery of dualism in the labor and product markets of the United States.[7]

Technological foundations of economic structure

The typologies of economic structure outlined in the preceding section are the subject of three quite distinct literatures. Nonetheless, there is a tendency to link them in discussion as if the secondary sector of the labor market were coincident with the small competitive firms of the periphery and these, in turn, were the vestiges of the traditional sector of an underdeveloped economy, while the modern parts of underdeveloped economies were part of the core economy of developed nations. As a political metaphor, this linkage has appeal, since it groups all the disadvantaged of the world and suggests, by association with the underdeveloped countries which served as colonies of industrialized nations, that they are products of neocolonialism. But the linkage is misleading. Disadvantaged workers often work in large enterprises, for example, in West Europe where automobile assembly is manned by immigrant labor. As Lisa Peattie suggested in underdeveloped countries, and as doctors, lawyers, and construction craftsmen make clear in our own, small firms frequently

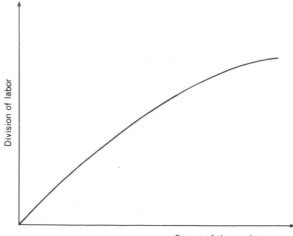

Extent of the market

Figure 1. *The division of labor and the extent of the market.*

occupy quite privileged positions in the labor market. But if the obvious linkage between these concepts is misleading, what precisely is the relationship between them? We propose here to understand that relationship by returning to the classical economic view of industrial technology.

The classical view of technology has been largely abandoned in modern economic theory. Contemporary theory has tried to define technology in terms of the combination of various factors of production, the choice of which is governed by relative factor prices. This has been true of the choice within a given set of known techniques of production, a problem for which there is a fully developed and generally accepted solution. It has also been true of the search for new techniques for production. There is no generally accepted solution to the latter problem, but virtually all recent efforts to solve it have taken the approach of relative factor prices.[8] The result is a view which inevitably depicts economic development as an accumulation of resources and has no way of dealing with the changes in the texture of economic activity and of daily life, which so obviously accompany the process.

Smith's theory of technology

The contemporary view represents a sharp departure from the classical tradition originating in the works of Adam Smith. In this earlier

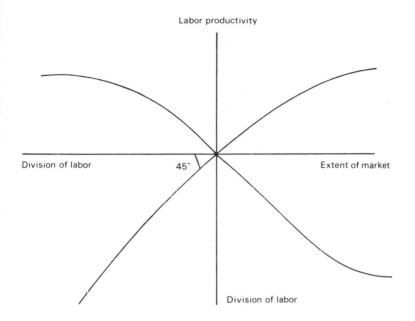

Figure 2. *The division of labor and the extent of the market: labor pro-*
ductivity.

tradition the forces commanding the evolution of technology lie outside the market; they are inherent in the nature of the technology
itself. In Smith's theory, these forces are captured by two basic postulates: that productivity (output per unit input) is an increasing function of the *division of labor*, and that the division of labor is limited by
the extent of the market.[9] Since per capita income is basically dependent upon productivity, income becomes a function of the division of
labor and the extent of the market, and income growth, or economic
development, thus becomes a process of expanding markets and dividing labor.

The thrust of this argument is illustrated by the curves in Figures 1
and 2. The relationships embodied in the diagrams are basically the
classical equivalent of the *production function* through which
growth is analyzed in modern theory. The relationships are more
far-reaching than the production function, because they have implications not only for the level of income but also for the structure of
production. To appreciate these implications, and to understand the
rationale for the basic postulates of Smith's theory, we have to consider the division of labor and the extent of the market.

For Smith, the notion of the division of labor is exemplified by his now classic pin factory, in which the process of the division of labor is carried to its ultimate conclusion. The work involved in the manufacture of pins has been broken down into a series of individual tasks, and each task is assigned to a single worker who performs it repeatedly. "One man draws out the wire, another straightens it, a third cuts it, a fourth points it, a fifth grinds it. . . ." This "modern" factory is contrasted to traditional craft production in which the whole pin is created by a single, skilled workman, who presumably completes each pin, performing the whole sequence of manufacturing operations, before moving on to the next. In our own times, the classic example of the division of labor is the automobile assembly line in which each worker does one operation in the assembly of the car. This case can be contrasted with certain experiments in "job enlargement" in which the car is assembled by a team of workers performing all (or at least a large cluster of) assembly tasks together. It can also be contrasted with prototype manufacture, where a single model is constructed by a group of craftsmen.

Smith argued that the division of labor contributed to productivity for three basic reasons: (1) improvements in worker dexterity because of increased concentration on a fewer number of tasks; (2) the saving in time which would be otherwise lost in moving from one task to another; and (3) "the application of machinery invented by workmen" who, in concentrating their attention on a single task, see opportunities for improvement which would otherwise be overlooked. Charles Babbage, who attempted to develop Smith's original idea, added a fourth, overarching factor: the principle of comparative advantage.[10] The principle, originally developed to explain the advantages of international trade, is that efficiency is maximized when each country, or worker, can concentrate on those tasks in which he or she has a relative advantage. All of these factors as explanations, at least of the extreme division of labor exemplified by the pin factory and the automobile assembly line, have recently been cast in doubt. We return to reexamine them later. For the moment, however, the argument presumes their validity.

Adam Smith's second postulate, that the division of labor is limited by the extent of the market, rests essentially upon the following idea. If *work* is thought of as divided into a set of tasks, an industry which produces one item a day might have one worker doing all of the tasks; if output expanded to two items, it could have two workers, each doing half the tasks; at three items, it would be three workers doing one-third of the tasks; and so on until each worker did a single task. (Since the rationale is increased productivity, the work day would get shorter, or output larger, with each division.) Obviously, the limit to this division of labor is the number of items produced, and this, in turn, depends on the extent of the market.

The optimal market from this point of view is, in other words, a market so large that each worker can be fully employed performing a single task. At the other extreme, with a very small market, each worker could be kept fully employed only by producing whole pins himself. Indeed, we can imagine a market for pins so small that a worker could not earn a living producing pins alone but would have to produce different products. In this sense, the extreme contrast to the pin factory is the subsistence economy in which the worker has to produce everything for himself. This is clearly also a situation of extremely low productivity and output. Thus, Smith's view of income growth and economic development implies a set of structural changes involving a progressive movement from a subsistence economy at one extreme to the pin factory at the other.

Smith seemed to think of the extent of the market in a geographic sense but, as the previous example suggests, what is involved in the concept of the "extent of the market" is the absolute number of items relative to the number of work tasks. The extent of the market in this sense of the term will increase with the level of income, and rising income levels will give rise to increasing productivity, a reversal of the direction of causality usually assumed. More important, in terms of the argument developed next, the extent of the market for an individual firm will depend upon the firm's absolute size, and productivity will thus automatically increase as the firm grows.

In addition to the extent of the market, we would add to Adam Smith's determinants of the division of labor three other factors: (1) the standardization of output, (2) the stability of the demand for output, and (3) the uncertainty of demand for output. The degree of standardization is partly a definitional matter. As we have defined the extent of the market, any given output or "bundle of goods" might range from one in which all items in the bundle were the same to one in which each item was different. Smith would say that in the former case the market was more extensive than in the latter. But we could equally well say that in the former case output was completely standard. The "degree of standardization" has connotations, however, that are not carried by "extensiveness." Thus, for example, the output of cars can be more or less standard depending upon the number of parts which different models have in common. Because of the importance of standardization, there is considerable interdependence among industries in the technology which each finds profitable to implement.

In terms of the argument of the current paper, the important additions to Smith's list are _stability_ and _certainty_. Stability will affect the division of labor in two ways. First, where demand is unstable and fluctuates, workers will be deployed from production during the downswing. A quick review of the list of factors favoring division of labor will indicate that the gains will be reduced when output, and by extension, employment, is intermittent. Thus, each level of instability in a given total output is equivalent, in terms of the profitable division of labor, to some smaller, stable level of output. Second, to the extent that the division of labor involves increased capital investment and capital is so specialized that it cannot transfer to other uses during troughs in demand, the periodic unemployment of capital which instability entails will also deter the division of labor. A similar argument can be made about the specialized labor skills which the division of labor seems to entail, provided there is some institutional mechanism which forces the unemployment of these skills to be accounted for in technological decisions.

The relationship between uncertainty and the division of labor follows from a similar set of considerations. Production schedules can be stabilized and economies of divisibility realized even in the face of instability in product demand through variations in inventories, but inventory investment will be discouraged when the fluctuations are unpredictable. People will not be willing to hold inventories when demand declines if the subsequent revival is problematic. Uncertainty will also discourage the investment in fixed capital which seems to accompany the division of labor.

In sum, Smith's argument suggests the following theory of technological development: Worker productivity is a function of the dexterity of the worker, of his capacity for innovation, of the time lost moving between tasks, and of the comparative advantages realized through the specialization of labor. Each of these is in turn a function of the division of labor. And the division of labor is a function of the extent of the market, the standardization of the product, and the stability and certainty of product demand.

Applications of economic processes

The basic relationship which we have been developing may be used to characterize at least three distinct phenomena. Smith himself used it to explain the increase of output for a given resource input, a process which might be termed *quantitative* economic growth for the economy as a whole. Secondly, the relationship may be used to trace the development of a single industry as it is born, grows to maturity, and then decays, and in this way can be extended to interpret the

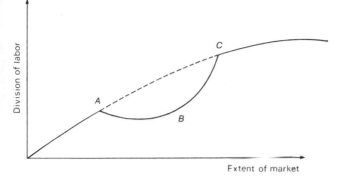

Figure 3. *The division of labor and the extent of the market: short-run and long-run adjustment paths.*

qualitative dimensions of economic growth in which the industrial composition of output shifts over time. Finally, the same basic relationship may be used to study the state of an industry at any given moment.

In characterizing quantitative economic growth, the relationship between the division of labor and the extent of the market may be interpreted as the growth path of the economy. The economy moves along this curve over time, and at any given moment is located at one point along it. We may further distinguish between long-run and short-run development. In the short run, the extension of the market may outrun the ability of the economy to exploit fully its benefits, particularly where these gains depend on innovative capital investment. The actual course of movement between any two points may thus be better approximated by the path ABC as in Figure 3.

Just as the economy transverses such a curve over time, so any single industry also does. For individual industries, however, growth is not unidirectional. At some point, industrial demand reaches a peak, and then begins to decline as substitutes are invented and economic growth shifts to other locations. Because much of the movement is irreversible, the decline of an industry would not take place on the same path along which it expanded, however, but rather along a higher, flatter path like that shown in Figure 4. The fact that it does so insures that economic growth is not solely an index number phenomenon. Without such irreversibility, in other words, it would be quite possible that the productivity gains in expanding industries simply compensated for the productivity losses in declining indus-

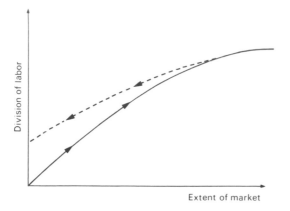

Figure 4. *The division of labor and the extent of the market: expansion and contraction paths.*

tries. But the former systematically outweigh the latter, because the relative prices in industries when they are expanding must almost by definition be higher than when they are contracting.

The third relationship which the curve may be said to illustrate is the state of a single industry at any moment. Products which are very similar in terms of their inputs and the character of their output and, except for differences in the division of labor, in the basic process through which they are produced, may exhibit substantial variations not only on the quantitative extent of the market but also in the degree of standardization and, even more important, in the stability and certainty of demand. Examples include the garment industry, whose products range from work clothes on one extreme to *haute couture* at the other. Restaurants run a similar gamut from short-order lunch counters, among which McDonald's is the extreme example of the division of labor, to *haute cuisine*. In most industries, the variation is probably continuous enough that we might think of the whole industry as being spread out along a path very similar to that traversed by its most *extended* component in its initial growth. The path along which the industry is spread will probably not, however, be the *same* as that along which the part located at the end point developed. Some of the innovations in the most extended part of the industry are likely to be applicable all along the line. This will be particularly true if, as is argued next, the division of labor is associated with the intellectual process of innovation. Hence, as the end point of a single industry

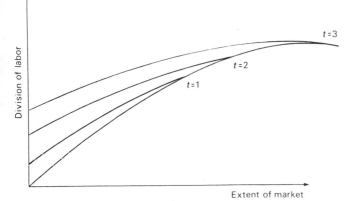

Figure 5. *The division of labor and the extent of the market: alternative time paths.*

moves outward, the curve along which the rest of the industry is located should shift upward as shown in Figure 5.

Dual product markets. The preceding theory of technological change may be applied directly to yield an explanation of a dual product market. The parts of the argument necessary to do so may be briefly summarized. They are Adam Smith's two basic postulates: (1) that productivity is dependent upon division of labor and (2) that the division of labor is a function of the size of the market. Two propositions have been added: (3) that the division of labor is also a function of the stability of demand (uncertainty works in the same way as instability but is not critical to the argument) and (4) that any product demand can be separated into a stable and an unstable portion, the two portions being separated by the floor to which demand falls at the trough of its cycle. (See dashed line in Figure 6.)

The critical elements in explaining a dual product market are Adam Smith's original postulates for the size of the firm. As long as productivity is solely dependent upon the division of labor and the division of labor depends *only* on the size of the market, each firm will face a declining average cost curve, that is, the larger its output, the smaller the unit cost of production. This means that any firms can cut costs by absorbing its competitors. It can, moreover, continue to cut costs until it is the only firm in the industry. Thus Adam Smith's

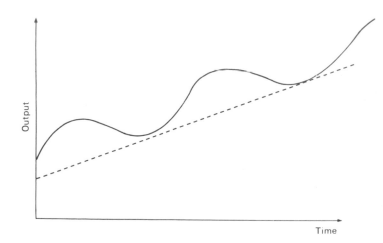

Figure 6. *The stabilization of production with fluctuating demand.*

theory of technology is one in which competition fares poorly, and this is undoubtedly one of the reasons it has received short shrift in modern economic theory, which draws heavily upon the competitive assumption.

The addition of stability to the theory as a determinant of the division of labor reduces the optimal size of the firm to something less than the size of the industry and, thus, restores the possibility of competition. But it does so only so long as the last proposition fails to hold. If demand can be compartmentalized into stable and unstable segments, the declining average cost curve will prevail for the stable segment and, in that segment, the theory implies that a single firm will emerge. Firms in the unstable segment will retain the traditional U-shaped average cost curve, and in that segment we could expect to find a number of much smaller firms.

Uncertainty has much the same effect as demand instability. Because, as noted earlier, if stable production can be maintained in the face of product demand by variations in inventories, it may be profitable for the large, or stable, sector of an industry to expand above the demand floor and into the fluctuating component. Such an expansion, however, will be deterred by uncertainty, which increases the risk that the firm will get stuck with excessive inventories.

This, then, constitutes the technological base for duality in the product market: large-scale enterprise with declining average cost curves catering to the predictable and largely stable segment of demand and much smaller scale firms with the traditional U-shaped average cost curves catering to the unpredictable and/or fluctuating portion of demand. Most of the characteristics of firms which Marris and Galbraith emphasize in their description of managerial capitalism and the new industrial state can be traced to their location in the stable segment of such a dual market. Such firms are capital intensive, because the stability and predictability of demand encourage investment in the fixed factor of production. They are preoccupied by growth, to the point where it seems to eclipse other managerial goals, because they face declining average cost curves and, hence, growth up to the limit of stable demand (and, if fluctuations are predictable, even beyond that limit) is always profitable. They would tend to be preoccupied by market share because market share is a good proxy for the stable portion of demand. The paradox, which their critics have emphasized, that both the firms and the authors who describe them should believe that they have controlled product demand when demand remains so obviously unstable and unpredictable, is explained by the fact that these firms have not attempted to control the whole of product demand but rather to *separate* from the rest that portion which lends itself to control. Arthur Moxham of DuPont put it:

> If we could by any measure buy out all competition and have an absolute monopoly in the field, it would not pay us. The essence of manufacture is steady and full product. The demand for the country for powder is variable. If we owned all therefore when slack times came we would have to curtail product to the extent of diminished demands. If on the other hand we control only 60% of it all and make that 60% cheaper than others, when slack times came we could still keep our capital employed to the *full*. . . .[11]

The theory does not yield a very satisfactory explanation for the number of firms in the stable sector: If average cost curves do indeed decline continuously, there should be only *one* such firm in each industry. The presence of *several* large firms suggests that perhaps the division of labor reaches a saturation point (at which point the average cost curve would level off and turn up). But it seems equally plausible that, when the number of firms in the stable portion becomes very small, further concentration is thwarted by antitrust legislation, cartel agreements, or tacit understandings generated by a mutual fear of the kind of competition which would be required to further reduce the number of enterprises.

All of this, it is to be noted, depends upon the proposition that demand can be segregated into a stable and an unstable portion. The technological theory which derives from Adam Smith only suggests that there are large economies in doing so. But these economies are *social* and in a market economy such as ours, they must somehow be privatized if they are to be realized. It is not easy to conceive of a single set of institutional arrangements which would permit this to happen. The way in which it happens, in practice, seems to vary substantially throughout the economy. Thus, in the automobile industry, the solution appears to be that the whole of product demand is controlled by the big three, who then segment production, building up an in-house capacity for the stable component and subcontracting the unstable component to a variety of smaller "parts" producers. In the machine tool industry, where the stable firms are smaller and more numerous than in the auto industry, the market seems to be segmented by a waiting period. As demand expands above the floor, the customers of the stable firms are forced to wait in line, and a variety of small job shops using highly skilled labor and substantially less specialized capital equipment grow up to meet the demand of those who become impatient with the waiting period. In the garment industry, the division seems to follow product lines more closely, the stable portion of demand being composed of, for example, work clothes and the unstable portion, women's dress clothes.

Two final notes about dualism in the modern economy: First, the peripheral sector need not be composed solely of firms catering to the unstable or uncertain portion of demand in a larger industry. There may also be a number of firms which, owing to the specific nature of the product or geographic differentiation or the like, simply have very small, albeit quite certain and stable markets. A number of household services as well as certain professional services fall into this category. The theory also suggests that new industries and declining industries will tend to resemble the peripheral sector.

Second, the theory need not imply that all peripheral firms will be similar; differences in the instability and uncertainty of the peripheral sector among industries may produce substantial variation in their technologies. The peripheral sector of some industries might even resemble the core sector of other industries in terms of its position on the division of labor curve.

Dualism which runs throughout a number of product markets is, like dualism in the labor market, probably less often a result of technology per se than of the tendency for different industries to find in the same institutional and legal arrangements a means of resolving the problem of separating demand into stable and unstable components.

The dual economy in economic development.   The dual product market in underdeveloped countries can be derived by using Smith's basic relationship between the division of labor and the extent of the market to represent the developmental path of an economy over time. The fact that the economy is basically underdeveloped implies that its domestic markets are small and that its own industries – those catering to the local market – will be found on the far left side of the curve. The modern sector, almost by definition, is located at some point on the far right of the curve. It is composed of enclave economies catering to a much larger metropolitan, or world market, and, by virtue of the much larger size of that market, consists of large, capital-intensive enterprise.

Definition of underdev.

This kind of underdeveloped dualism, it should be noted, resembles the dualism in developed economies because both derive from the same underlying relationships, those among the extent of the market, the division of labor, and productivity, but the causes of dualism here are different. In the underdeveloped case, it is the existence of different *industries* with *markets of very different sizes*; in the case of developed economies, it is the existence within the same industry of *markets* with *very different degrees of stability*.

?

As the underdeveloped economy develops, it should begin to generate the kind of dualism associated with the modern economy, and the importance of the traditional sources of dualism should decline. We can imagine, however, a number of ways in which the two sources of dualism might interact with each other. The small institutions of the traditional sector might, for example, simply shift their function to that of handling the unstable portion of demand in a modern economy; or they might disappear completely and be replaced by a new set of modern (but peripheral) firms. In subsequent chapters, Berger examines how France and Italy have made special efforts to preserve the traditional sector through state subsidies, and the modern sector has utilized the political power of the traditional sector to support its own dualistic structure.

The dual labor market. To translate this argument about the structure of technologies into one about the structure of the labor market, two intermediate steps are required: to explore the relationship between the job structure and the structure of the labor market; next, to analyze the relationship between the division of labor and the structure of jobs.

Job structure and labor market structure. The basic argument here is that the labor market stratum in which a particular job is located depends upon the number of tasks of which it is composed and the relationship among those tasks. Jobs involving a wide variety of tasks, which are, nonetheless, related to each other in some way, will be found in the upper tier of the primary sector. Jobs involving a narrow range of tasks, or a range of tasks which, while relatively wide, has no obvious common elements will be found in the lower tier of the primary sector. Jobs involving very few tasks, or tasks that are diverse and unstable, will be found in the secondary sector.

The hypotheses rest upon the notion, introduced in presenting the expanded concept of labor market stratification, that the characteristics of different strata are, at root, an expression of different modes of learning and understanding work. A wide range of interrelated work tasks is conducive to the abstract modes of learning and understanding. This, we argued, identifies the upper tier of the primary sector. A relatively narrow range of tasks and/or task diversity is conducive to the concrete mode, which characterizes the lower tier. In the secondary sector, work is directed and coordinated through the supervisor and is not dependent upon the skill or understanding of the work force. Hence, work which is either extremely simple or, because of its variety and instability, defies easy understanding tends to fall into this category.

Two distinct explanations can be offered as to why tasks should be related to modes of understanding in this way. The first is an argument about the economics of learning and would explain the structure of labor markets in a social system where the learning process is governed by an economic calculus. The basic difference between concrete and abstract learning, from an economic point of view, is that the former is a variable cost process while the latter is a fixed cost process. The cost of concrete learning is a function of the *number of tasks* learned and increases progressively as the number of tasks rises. Think, for example, of memorizing the tasks involved in assembly of a car. Abstract learning is not of this kind. There is presumably a certain, relatively high cost of learning the basic abstractions (e.g., the car and how it operates), but once learned, the abstraction will cover all the relevant tasks. The different cost functions are graphed in Figure 7. As can be seen by glancing at that figure, the least cost mode of learning will depend upon the number of tasks involved.

Figure 7, of course, oversimplifies the problem. The most important (but not the only) respect in which it does so is the assumption, upon which the diagram is based, that the cost of learning is solely dependent upon the number of tasks involved. Other aspects of the tasks may also be influential. One abstraction may not cover all tasks. If the tasks are extremely diverse, several abstractions, or high levels of abstractions which are more difficult and hence more costly to learn, will be required to understand them. For this reason, the diversity

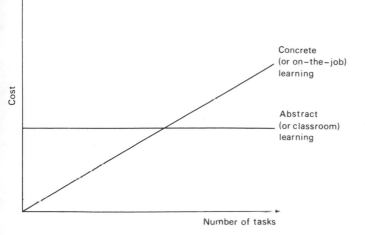

Figure 7. *Concrete and abstract learning.*

among tasks, as well as the number, becomes a determinant of the market stratum into which a job is likely to fall.

The same propositions may be derived from a set of psychological assumptions which are not dependent upon the notion that learning is subject to a cost calculus. The basic notion here is that there is a natural progression in the understanding of experiences.[19] All experience initially seems chaotic and is first ordered, to the extent it is ordered at all, in relationship to individual personalities, as is the case with work experience in the secondary sector. The fact that human experience is generated in some systematic way insures that most experience will be repeated and pattern itself into recurrent relationships with the external environment. As it does so, we develop the kinds of concrete understandings of that experience characteristic of the lower tier of the primary sector. At this stage, however, we are still unable to perceive the systems which are actually generating those experiences. As the amount of experience broadens and the range of diversity increases still further, however, we are eventually able to see, in the case of at least some of what we experience in our lives, the broad principles out of which they grow and when this perception develops, we have the abstract understanding which prevails in the upper tier. These are natural stages which people appear to pass through as they mature from infant to adult. But, as adults, we operate at all levels of understanding. Some of our experiences are understandable in abstract terms; others in a concrete way; still others seem to be the product of random (chaotic) events. Again, how we perceive things will obviously depend not simply upon the amount of experience we are attempting to organize but also upon the stability of the environment in which it occurs (since that will facilitate concrete understanding) and the diversity of experience over the range which any governing principle might explain (since diversity will facilitate abstraction).

The thrust of this interpretation is that, whatever the cost of learning, it would be very difficult for an assembly line worker who does three operations on a car, to think of his job in terms of an "automobile" and equally difficult for a craftsman, who assembles the whole car, to memorize his job and think of what he does as just a very long list of operations which he has learned by rote and performs one after another.

Neither the psychological nor the economic interpretations imply a strict relationship between job tasks and labor market structure. Both suggest a number of other variables. Essentially unskilled jobs can, for example, be joined to lines of progression, or careers, which lead to more highly skilled positions, and the ethos and organization of production can encourage or discourage workers with multitask jobs to perceive the broad, technical principles which underlie them. This range of indeterminacy would provide ample opportunity, in the actual structuring of the market, for the play of the kinds of political and institutional factors upon which the previous chapter focused.

The division of labor and the job structure.   The final step in translating Adam Smith's theory of the division of labor into a theory of labor market structure is an argument about the relationship between the division of labor and the distribution of jobs by the number of tasks which the jobs entail. Smith's own views about the division of labor have fairly definite implications for the beginning and end of this process. The job distribution, at the beginning, they imply, would consist exclusively of highly skilled, multitask jobs as pictured in Figure 8. As we have just argued, jobs of this kind would tend to fall in the upper tier. The pin factory example implied that at the end point of the process, the job distribution would consist of elemental, single task jobs. Such jobs can be learned quickly and involve very little skill at all. To this extent, they can potentially fall into the secondary labor market. Smith himself has very little to say about the intermediate stages of the process. Presumably, jobs in these stages consist of clusters of tasks, broad enough to require a certain amount of learning to

Figure 8. *Initial stage of the division of labor.*

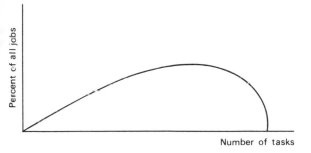

Figure 9. *Intermediate stage of the division of labor.*

develop proficiency but sufficiently narrow and routinized that abstract understanding is neither required nor encouraged. But we can imagine this occurring in ways which continue to preserve a large number of highly skilled, multitask jobs for a long period of time (as pictured in Figure 9) or alternatively in ways which quickly split up such jobs (as pictured in Figure 10), creating many lesser skilled jobs in their place.

Ultimately, the impact of the division of labor upon the job structure is an empirical question and one that has never been systematically investigated. The available evidence, fragmentary as it is, suggested two amendments to the view just articulated. First, work at relatively early stages in the division of labor involves a number of essentially unskilled tasks which can be assigned to separate groups of workers. These workers need no real understanding of the job – either in abstract terms or as routine – and can be in the secondary sector. Second, at later stages in the division of labor, precisely be-

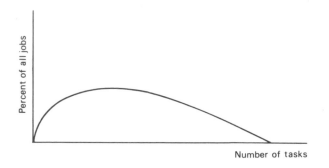

Figure 10. *Late stage of the division of labor.*

cause the workers themselves have so little real understanding of the processes in which they are involved, a separate group of workers is required to "manage" the production process, insuring coordination and handling nonroutine situations. The end point of the process as envisaged by Smith in the pin factory example is thus not the whole story.

It is not clear, however, that the historical evolution of the job structure can be captured simply by amending Smith's model. A series of questions are raised by Adam Smith's view of the division of labor, which are most serious with respect to the pin factory, and the relationship between the division of labor and the job structure which the example seems to imply. The most prominent attack is that of Stephen Marglin.[13] Marglin examines each of the three basic reasons which Smith adduces for the division of labor and argues that none seems sufficient to justify that type of organization in the pin factory. The argument about the workman's propensity to innovate is refuted by Smith himself, who argues elsewhere in *The Wealth of Nations* that prolonged concentration on excessively fragmented tasks produces mental dullness and lethargy.[14] Marglin points out that Smith's two other factors – the saving of set-up time and increased dexterity – can be obtained without anything like complete fragmentation. The addition of comparative advantage to the list of factors does not seem to overcome these difficulties, since the jobs which Smith was attempting to justify are so trivial that differences among workers in terms of ability to learn one as opposed to another are probably insignificant. Marglin's skepticism about Smith's rationale is buttressed by a number of experiments in job enlargement.[15] The experiments have not produced the clear results which the proponents of job enlargement would have liked but their very inconclusiveness is as damning to Smith's argument as it is to that of his doctrinaire opponents. The experiments have clearly shown that there are savings to be had in job enlargement – both in the greater engagement of labor force in the conscious work process and in the elimination of lower level managerial officials, who are required to monitor and coordinate the production process in a fragmented work situation (where the workers themselves neither see the relationship among tasks nor are sufficiently engaged in what they are doing to be able to control it). While these savings may not be sufficient to make the enlarged jobs clearly more efficient than the fragmented job structure, they are more than enough to undermine the case for the latter which Smith originally constructed.

An alternative rationale for the division of labor

If Smith's original understanding for the division of labor cannot be sustained, however, it can be interpreted in a very different way as part of the intellectual process in technological development. This interpretation will support the arguments about the economic structure already developed, but it is not subject to the same objections. It is, moreover, much more consonant with contemporary notions of the technological development which accompanies these structural changes as the embodiment of new ideas or, in other words, "scientific progress." And it seems to capture the spirit of the notion of innovation as "discovery," whereas Smith's model seems to imply that technological change is merely the playing out of known relationships which economic conditions would not previously support. Finally, such an interpretation has the additional advantage of paralleling the interpretation of market structure as involving variation across strata in the way in which people learn and understand their work.

Under this alternative interpretation of technological change, the process of economic development is essentially one of producing a larger and more various output from the same basic resources, and it is predicated on the development of new *ideas* about the way in which the resources can be utilized. In the sense that basic resources are the "elements" of production, development involves the continual recombination of those elements in new and different ways. This recombination can be thought of as first and foremost an intellectual process, the process of the invention and discovery of new ideas. In this process, however, the *old* ideas embodied in existing production processes constitute a tremendous obstacle. They do so because of the hold which they have upon the imagination. To the extent that we are accustomed to seeing the elements of the production process combined in given ways and that we understand the elements in those terms, it becomes very difficult to conceive alternatives. To develop alternative conceptions we have to separate the elements of production from the process in which they are engaged and perceive them independently, then, reorganize and recombine them in novel and original forms. The division of labor as Smith describes it becomes the process through which the existing productive organization is broken down and separated into its component elements, the process through which we escape the intellectual grip of existing forms of organization. But this process, which we might speak of as *fragmentation* or *decomposition,* is only a part of the division of labor in the broadest sense. The second part is the *recombination* or *synthesis* of the elements of production through an invention or discovery. And development actually involves a kind of alternation or dialectic, moving back and forth between *decomposition* and *recombination,* between *fragmentation* and *synthesis.* The process in total is typified by the way in which one manufacturing engineer interviewed in a recent study described the relationship between the division of labor in the Smithian sense of the term and mechanization.[16] For him, what was important about the kind of fragmentation involved in the pin factory was that it enabled him to take each individual element and think of it in terms of the logic of machinery. Until the element is separated in this way, it is very difficult to mechanize it, because the thinking about it is dominated either by the logic of human activity or by the logic of the product which goes into producing it.

The basic proposition is also illustrated by another, more artificial, but possibly more telling example: the movement from craft to mass production. In craft production, for example, of a carriage, the craftsman produces the carriage on order from a customer, delivers it, and is paid. In mass production, each operation of production and sale occurs in a series of simple tasks. Once broken down in this way, it is possible to see that certain tasks (for example, the initial ordering, the purchase of raw materials, and the final sale) have a logic very different from the actual production of the carriage. When produced by the craftsman, these operations occur at such widely different points in time that their relationship is likely to be obscured by a preoccupation with production and go unnoticed. But once distinguished, they can be regrouped into a marketing or accounting department. The marketing and accounting functions can in turn be divided and fragmented. Once this occurs, it will become apparent that certain operations involve numerical calculations which can be assigned to a computer department, and so on.

This alternative rationale for the division of labor has very similar implications for the structure of enterprises to that of Adam Smith's. The market must be large enough to support the specialization which the division of labor entails and to keep the specialized components of the production process fully employed. And, for this same reason, the process will also be responsive to the other variables identified in the earlier discussions, the standardization of the product, the stability and certainty of demand for the product, and the durability of the product itself.

The alternative rationale for the division of labor does, however, have somewhat different implications for the impact of that process on the job structure. If the process is essentially intellectual, why must it be physically embodied in the production process itself? A certain amount of task differentiation within the actual process might be helpful to the engineer in visualizing the distinctions which he must draw in order to innovate, but the degree of fragmentation exemplified by the pin factory hardly seems to be required. Moreover, even if it did imply such fragmentation, that fragmentation and the consequent movement of the distribution of jobs toward the unskilled end of the spectrum would only be half the story. At the same time, and indeed as an outgrowth of fragmentation, there is a process of recombination and synthesis that is recreating whole jobs at the other end of the spectrum. Hence, however accurate Smith's description might be for the job structure of older industries, it is not a fruitful description of the structure of the economy as a whole.

Even though the organization of the pin factory is not inherent in the division of labor, it does appear that in older industries the work which is not (or has not yet been) resynthesized into new activities will become increasingly less comprehensible on its face and hence increasingly less easy to understand in abstract forms. As more and more elements are removed from the process and performed outside in separate accounting departments, for example, or embodied in the operation of a machine, the tasks which remain to be performed by labor must appear to those performing them as increasingly disconnected. And this is indeed the case in the sense that what remains behind is essentially a residual, a set of operations which were once obviously related to each other through the logic of the old production process but which are now united only by the fact that they have not yet been integrated into something else. To understand the relationship among them, one must know the history of the technology. This is, of course, not impossible to know or to learn, but it is not something which can be learned on the job. Thus, in sum, the division of labor seems to imply that work which is not synthesized becomes increasingly difficult to conceive on the job in holistic terms. In this sense, it becomes increasingly conducive to the modes of understanding which prevail in the lower tier of the labor market. At the same time, the craft learning process, in which abstract understanding derives from the accumulation of specific task knowledge on the job, is progressively foreclosed. The range of tasks is so diminished by the process of synthesis that it first becomes more difficult and ultimately becomes impossible to see the operation of a single coherent logic in what remains. Thus, to the extent that abstract understanding is required to coordinate the production process, it must be obtained in the classroom. And, to the extent that the crafts constitute a kind of intermediate position between the abstract approach of the upper tier and the concrete approach of the lower tier, fragmentation would appear to imply an increasing polarity. Finally, it is probably true that the net result of these effects is to reduce the relative cost of organizing work in the highly fragmented fashion exemplified by the pin factory. The process of distinguishing the individual tasks for intellectual purposes obviously yields, almost as a by-product, the basic vision required to design the pin factory and the changing character of on-the-job experience must reduce the relative cost of training the kind of dichotomous labor force which the pin factory involves. But there is nothing here to suggest that the changes in relative cost will *necessarily* be such as to make the pin factory cost dominant, and we can well imagine that the actual job structure will come to depend upon the kind of factors which Marglin emphasized in his argument.

Alternative views of dualism

What is the relationship between the views of dual labor markets as a response to the flux and uncertainty developed in the first chapter and the process of the division of labor which we have developed here? The question can be answered by focusing upon the role of flux and uncertainty in that process. Such instability has the effect in the schema we have just outlined of limiting the market. The benefits in productive efficiency which are generated by the division of labor can be appropriated by society only if the specialized productive resources are fully employed. If this is not possible, and the employment of those resources fluctuates widely, then the gains from specialization are simply dissipated in sustaining the specialized resources in their periods of unemployment, and the productive unit could do better by using a less highly articulated division of labor, that is, polivariate resources which are capable of moving about from one kind of task to another. This choice tends to lead to a separation of the market for any commodity into (1) a stable component that is met through a relatively extensive division of labor, utilizing highly specialized resources and (2) an unstable component, where production involves a less highly articulated division of labor, which utilizes capital and labor that are less specialized and consequently capable of moving back and forth with fluctuations in demand among a variety of different activities.

We can thus conceive of the relationship between instability and industrial society in two distinct ways. In one conception, upon which the argument of the first chapter has built, instability and its distribution is a common problem of industrial society and tends to lead to dichotomies in the social structure as individual groups or larger social classes attempt to build shelters against its impact. In the second conception, industrial society is characterized by the process of the division of labor, and instability is a variable affecting that process. This view also leads us to expect dichotomies in the social and economic structure, but dichotomies associated with pressures in the system toward economic efficiency and the attempt of producers to extract a relatively stable and predictable component of demand, where production can utilize the most advanced division of labor, from the fluctuating component of demand which can be met profitably only with less specialized resources.

Are these two explanations and the dichotomies to which they lead congruent? Yes and no. No, in the sense that one is basically distributional, the other is essentially technological. They are thus responsive to different political dynamics. Since the two push in more or less the same direction, we would expect them to interact and reenforce each other; but they do have different implications for the end result, and hence it will matter how the two processes are put together and which dominates. To the extent that the division of labor dominates, we would expect to find the two sectors of the market operating with different technologies and different organizational structures but not necessarily with different labor force groups. To the extent that the end result is dominated by the policies of distribution, the technologies in the two sectors will not necessarily be different: the differences will tend rather to reflect differences in the power of the groups who operate in the two sectors.

But, at another level of analysis, the two processes are not completely independent, and we can speak of a certain congruence: The process of the division of labor aggravates the problem of instability and uncertainty in economic activity and, in so doing, increases the significance of any arrangement which distributes its impact. It has this effect because it involves, per force, increased specialization, and hence it enhances the dependence among units in the productive process for their economic validity and significance. This is readily seen by comparison with a primitive, subsistence economy. In such an economy, most productive units are capable of engaging in a number of different activities. Presumably, this limits their capacity in any one "trade," but it also limits their dependence upon their trade for their livelihood. If it rains, they perform indoor work rather than outdoor work; if the cow dies, there is still the goat; if the wheat crop fails, there is barley. The characterization of industrial society in terms of the division of labor implies that it is a society in which people are, relative to the primitive model, much more highly specialized and becoming more so. It also implies that the greater productivity and high incomes which industrialism offers derive from this specialization. Because people and other productive re- sources are specialized, the range of activities which they can perform is limited, and this makes instability and uncertainty an increasingly severe problem. It is not simply that people specialize in activities: The people who raise cows are different from the people who raise goats; those who grow wheat are distinct from those who grow barley. But within a speciality, there are specialities: There are those who milk the cow and those who tend to breeding; those who take care of the cow when it is sick; others who take over when it is dead. The livelihood of people under such a system is obviously sensitive, not only to the demand for cows but also to the number of calves which are born, the number of cows which become sick, the number of sick cows which die. And it is this sensitivity which generates the politics of economic security in industrial society. In this sense, the distribu- tional aspect of instability is intimately tied up with the technological.

Ultimately, of course, the two aspects of uncertainty remain dis- tinct. They are not congruent; only derive from common origins. But the fact is extremely important because they almost invariably appear together and in the political process get intertwined. It is only by reference to this common origin that the analyst will be able to iden- tify these two forces as distinct and begin to identify their separate effects. The need and possibility of doing this is the basic case for an approach to industrial society which concentrates upon a *process* as its defining characteristic, as opposed to a common set of *problems* to which it is the response.

NOTES

1. Robert Averitt, *The Dual Economy* (New York: Norton, 1968).
2. Robin Marris, *The Economics of Managerial Capitalism* (New York: The Free Press, 1964).

3. John Kenneth Galbraith, *The New Industrial State* (Boston: Houghton Mifflin, 1967).
4. See, for example, Robert M. Solow, "The New Industrial State or Son of Affluence," *The Public Interest* (Fall 1967), no. 9, 100–8.
5. See, for example, Julius H. Boeke, *Economics and Economic Policies of Real Societies, as Exemplified by Indonesia* (New York: International Secretariat, Institute of Pacific Relations, 1953). But also, Benjamin H. Higgins, *Economic Development: Principles, Problems and Policies* (New York: Norton, 1968).
6. Lisa Peattie, *The "Informal Sector" and "Marginality," Some Dualistic Concepts in the Light of Field Research*, M.I.T., mimeo., 1978.
7. See also Suzanne Berger, "The Uses of the Traditional Sector: Why the Declining Classes Survive," in F. Bechhofer and B. Elliott, *The Petty Bourgeoisie* (London: Macmillan, 1980).
8. See, for example, Paul A. Samuelson, "A Theory of Induced Innovation Along Kennedy–Weisacker Lines," *Review of Economics and Statistics*, 47 (November 1965), 343–56.
9. Adam Smith, *The Wealth of Nations* (New York: Modern Library, 1937), pp. 3–21, (Book 1, Chs. 1–3).
10. Charles Babbage, *On the Economy of Machinery and Manufacturers* (New York: Augustus Kelley, 1963), pp. 225–6.
11. Alfred Dupont Chandler, *The Visible Hand, The Managerial Revolution in American Business* (Cambridge, Mass.: Belknap Press, 1977), p. 442.
12. See Hans G. Furth, *Piaget and Knowledge: Theoretical Foundations* (Englewood Cliffs, N.J.: Prentice Hall, 1969).
13. Stephen A. Marglin, "What Do Bosses Do? The Origins and Functions of Hierarchy in Capitalist Production," *The Review of Radical Political Economics*, 6 (Summer 1974), no. 2, 60–112, esp. p. 66.
14. Smith, *Wealth of Nations*, pp. 734–5.
15. See, for example, Louis E. Davis and Albert B. Cherns, *The Quality of Working Life, Vol. II Cases and Commentary* (New York: The Free Press, 1975).
16. Michael J. Piore, "The Impact of the Labor Market Upon the Design and Selection of Productive Techniques Within the Manufacturing Plant," *Quarterly Journal of Economics*, 82 (November 1968), 602–20.

PART TWO

A POLITICAL APPROACH

The chapters in Part Two focus upon the politics of segmentation. The structure parallels that of the preceding section. Chapter 4, like Chapter 2, looks at particular dualistic structures: It examines the specific political and social forces which work to create and recreate patterns of segmentation in France and Italy. Chapter 5 moves toward a general theory: It lays out the assumptions upon which dualism might be incorporated into a theory of the interaction between politics and socioeconomic structure in industrial society. It argues that new departures in political theory, analogous to those which Chapter 3 urges in economic theory, are required to account for those discontinuities as integral features of industrial societies and to escape the conception of such structures as anomolies implicit in liberal and Marxist thought.

The political explanations of dualism developed in these chapters relate to the economic explanations in the chapters which precede them in three ways. First, politics in the broad sense accounts for the particular types of segmentation which emerge in various industrial societies. Even if economic analysis could provide a sufficient account of the thrust to dualism, as Chapter 3 implies, the problem would still remain of explaining the particular forms of dualism in different countries. Perhaps some national differences might be explained by expanding the theory of the national division of labor to one of the international division of labor. But even in such a theory, we would argue that it is the politics of nations which equips given countries to play particular economic roles in that division as much as their resource endowments or other technical traits. And certainly, to retain the notion of an economic process which generates common and universal constraints, as Piore develops the argument in the preceding chapters, the explanation of differentiation must rest on other extraeconomic factors, that is, politics, culture, history, society.

Secondly, economic analysis does not provide a sufficient account

85

of the origins of dualism, because politics is an autonomous source of the problems that industrial societies deal with by preserving and creating segmentation or dualism. Thus as we shall show in the following chapters, the attempts of various political groups to control the sources of political instability in their societies may lead them to support dualism, even when to do so requires major economic sacrifices. The functions that dualism performs in the maintenance of political stability and social order provide many reasons for the decisions and policies that work to reproduce it (apart from the economic advantages that various other groups in society may perceive in the structures of segmentation).

Finally, in addition to accounting for the emergence and reproduction of alternative forms of segmentation, politics is critical for understanding whether the differences among alternative forms are significant. It is only by reference to national politics and to the impact, through politics, of dualism on various groups that we can determine whether a particular structural variant is indeed an important and significant aspect of national life or merely a minor twist upon a theme common to all industrial societies. Only a political analysis can tell us what difference it makes – for the groups involved, for national politics, for economics – that in Italy dualism relies heavily on the employment of its own citizens in terms that vary according to whether the job is located in the large-scale, capital-intensive, unionized segment of the economy or in the small-scale, labor-intensive, less-organized segment, whereas in France dualism now depends heavily on the employment throughout the economy of foreigners from less-developed nations. Similarly, the importance of dualism in the analysis of the American labor market, which Piore develops in his essays, emerged only after race, which is critical to the form which dualism takes in the United States, had become an issue in national political life.

The next chapters explore these three lines of argument in the following ways. Chapter 4 offers first a political interpretation of the particular solutions that emerged in France and Italy as groups sought to escape economic uncertainty and in the process transferred the costs of their own increased security to other, more vulnerable groups. Then the chapter identifies the specifically political considerations that lead even those powerful modern groups for whom dualism entails heavy economic costs to consent to its survival. This argument about the autonomous political sources of dualism proceeds on the basis of assumptions about the politics of industrial societies and about the trajectory along which these societies are moving that diverge in important respects from those on which Marxist and liberal theories are built. The final chapter develops the claim that the Marxist and liberal failures to account for the discontinuities that appear in mature industrial states have general significance for a theory of the politics of the industrial world. To understand the politics of these countries, to analyze the axes of conflict and alliance along which transformation takes place, to spell out the real range of alternative solutions for the common problems these societies face – all require incorporating in the center of our conception of an industrial society the discontinuities that conventional views have obscured.

One final introductory point. The political analysis in the next chapters focuses on a particular aspect of dualism: the traditional sector. Here we consider the economic and political functions in advanced industrial societies of a class of small, independent property owners – shopkeepers, farmers, small and medium businessmen – whose very survival appears problematic in the conventional theories of modern society. To account both for the persistence on a significant scale of this segment of the economy and also for its renewal (even its expansion) requires looking at the political and economic relationships that link these enterprises and social classes to the most advanced sectors of the society. The traditional sector survives not simply because of the vestigial power of its numbers but because of the ways in which its political and economic interests overlap with those of the modern sector.

To distinguish between traditional and modern sectors does not imply that the former is made up of old units and the latter of new ones. Indeed, many of the firms that we call traditional are of recent creation. What is critical is that this form of dualism appears only in societies with particular historical and political resources. The template with which these societies distinguish between traditional and modern firms and social classes is one they bring into current affairs from the past. The past has been crystallized in the structures of the economy, in patterns of social and political alliance, in laws that identify these groups as a universe subject to particular kinds of regulation, in ideologies that attribute to them special virtues or dangers. Thus when new firms appear in the traditional sector, they find available forms of protection and prestige that the sector has enjoyed in the past; at the same time, they are constrained by operating in the old molds. In brief, the pattern of segmentation based on traditional enterprises allows us to see how politics and history cast out both the problems that contemporary societies face and the resources with which societies organize to meet those problems.

4

THE TRADITIONAL SECTOR IN FRANCE AND ITALY

In the calculations of scholars and politicians alike, the last days of traditional groups in modern industrial societies have long ago been counted. Whether from the perspective of theorists of political development or from that of the elites of advanced industrial societies, the remnants of traditional society and economy are in the final stages of withering away. Industrial concentration, technological innovation, the expansion of markets, the economies of scale of large units – all these factors and more make the productivity and profitability of large, modern, capital-intensive firms ever greater than that of small, traditional enterprise. At the same time, the processes of social, cultural, and political modernization that accompany industrialization have eroded the bases of traditional life.

In the most widely held views of industrial societies, traditional groups are seen as engaged in rearguard political battles that win temporary reprieves. But aging and generational turnover will inevitably finish off what economic competition has already rendered vestigial. Even these conventional explanations recognize that the numbers of small, familial enterprises in many advanced industrial societies remain significant; also, that these firms receive legislative protection and subsidies that cushion the impact of competition and thereby secure a longer lease on life. But what is significant about the numbers is that they are falling. And what explains the state's role in maintaining the traditional sector is an electoral motivation that will disappear as these numbers continue to fall. Conflicts of interests between traditional and modern groups in advanced industrial societies are, in this perspective, no more than the last echoes of a struggle whose outcome was long ago decided. Skirmishes continue, for old generations die out slowly. Though defeated, the passive weight of their numbers assures them a veto power in politics and the economy. But it makes little difference whether it is on one issue or another that the traditional groups score a victory; since their strength is only residual, it can at most be temporary.

Regarded from this perspective, any one of the traditional survivals in Western European societies can be seen as enjoying the last gasp of life before inevitable demise. That they are alive at all can be attributed to the relative efficacy of the artificial resuscitation that state protection provides. The prediction of ultimate withering away can never be disproved so long as the final moment can be indefinitely, albeit "temporarily," extended.

And yet, however difficult to refute directly, this theory of the last gasp of the traditional sector, with all its implications for the vestigial character of the groups that remain, has become less and less satisfactory. Looking across the various sectors and activities that might be considered traditional, considering together the hundreds of apparently unrelated skirmishes of recent decades – over the expansion of supermarkets, over agricultural subsidies for small farmers, over industrial structures, over state credit and social security systems, and so forth – we see a pattern of survival that suggests that the role of the traditional sector in modern societies is far more important than we have understood.

In the "withering-away" paradigm, disappearance of the traditional sector is the fact that can be systematically analyzed and predicted, while survival must be treated as temporary, accidental, and without consequences. In contrast, in the now perspective we will suggest, the survival of the traditional sector and its role today can be seen as the result of certain inherent features and tensions of advanced industrial societies. The facts of resilience, adaptation, and reproduction of traditional groups appear in this view as centrally related to the social, economic, and political functions that the traditional sector plays in contemporary societies. The cases of survival, the political victories of traditional groups, the willingness of the political elites and of the powerful groups in the modern sector of the economy to pay high costs for protecting the traditional remnants – all these are no longer to be seen as marginal, circumstantial, and transitional phenomena, but rather as parts of a larger pattern.

The evidence of a systematic relationship among the traditional survival cases, on the one hand, and between them and key structures and processes of modern society, on the other, falls into three general categories. First, the numbers of traditional firms, the proportion of the population employed in them, and the shifts in these numbers reflect a persistence and a responsiveness to needs of the modern sector that cannot be adequately explained by the usual theories of decline. Secondly, far from being vestigial to the operation of the most advanced sectors of society, the traditional groups appear to perform critical functions in maintaining and permitting the expansion of the modern sector. Third, the survival of the traditional sector appears to be both natural and willed; that is, it is the product of inertia – the slowness of generational turnover – and of the economic advantages that modern firms find in using traditional firms for a variety of purposes; and it is also the result of deliberate political choices and decisions to preserve traditional firms.

The evidence that we will present to develop and support each of these three lines of argument has been drawn from France and Italy, both countries with traditional sectors of considerable magnitude. That we should find the traditional sector playing a significant part in the politics and economy of these countries is all the more revealing because they represent precisely the kinds of cases that the conventional theories of decline should explain, if the theories are to hold. France is, by any measure, one of the most advanced industrial societies, with until recently one of the highest growth rates and per capita gross national products in Western Europe. Italy is the very model of a backward society rapidly catching up with the rest of industrial Europe. France and Italy are, moreover, not at all unique in the ways that they have preserved and used their traditional sectors, and we could as well include evidence from much of the rest of Western Europe and Japan.[1] Indeed, the cases of advanced industrial states without significant traditional sectors are the exception, and in them, other groups – blacks, foreign workers, or women – appear to perform the functions that in France and Italy are dealt with by resort to the traditional sector.

A census of the traditional sector

Definitions

The difficulties of surveying the traditional sector in industrial societies are from the outset compounded by the problem of definition, for which there does not seem to be any entirely satisfactory solution. No single variable can be strictly identified with traditionalism; or rather, narrowly specified definitions of the traditional sector pick out a small number of groups and firms whose behaviors, structure, and evolution cannot be explained without treating them as part of a much larger, albeit less precisely bounded, population. For this reason, traditionalism in contemporary societies seems best understood when explored with a rather loose definition, with shifting boundaries and a core population specified by several overlapping characteristics.

For the purposes of the general argument here, the two critical dimensions of traditionalism are economic and political. From an economic point of view, traditional groups are those whose activities involve the production of goods with technologies, costs, capital–labor ratios, and patterns of ownership and management that are significantly different from those used in the production of the same goods by other, modern firms. In the complex of differences that distinguishes a traditional from a modern firm, no one variable is determining; rather, we must consider various converging and overlapping factors: small firm size, higher labor–capital ratios, specific market relations, lower productivity, family ownership, and particular strategies and styles of management. Small firm size is highly correlated with all these variables, and in defining traditional economic firms, we are above all describing the class of small, independent, property owners: farmers, shopkeepers, artisans, and certain small and medium businessmen.[2]

While this definition has the advantage of focusing on the anomaly we seek to explain – namely, the survival on a large scale in an advanced industrial economy of groups that produce goods and services in ways systematically different and putatively less efficient than others – it is in other respects too restrictive. For example, we might wish to include in a definition of traditional economic activity those firms that make particular kinds of traditional goods or offer traditional services such as blacksmiths or artisanal shoemakers. Since these firms are producing different products for different markets than the modern firms, it is virtually impossible to catch them in the same definitional net, for there is no way of comparing productivity, efficiency, and technologies. Indeed, in affluent societies, the growing desire for handmade goods and for specialized and personalized services has led to a proliferation of producers and goods of a "traditional" sort, and yet the Harvard Square sandal maker can hardly be considered traditional. Because of problems of this sort, it seems better to build analytically on the cases of firms producing the same goods and services in different ways and only after that to include some part of the firms making different products.

Another kind of difficulty is raised for the definition by the case of those large firms that are less productive, more labor intensive, or more "traditionally" managed than others of their size in the same branch. Should size alone exclude them from the group we consider traditional? If the boundaries of the traditional sector were to be drawn wholly on economic criteria, there would seem to be no reason to do so. In fact, the economic dimensions of the sector are conditioned by political and social factors in ways that make a strictly economic definition inadequate.

The traditional sector is carved out of a large domain of economic facts by social perceptions and values and by political decisions. Which firms are traditional and which modern reflects social choices as much as it does any given economic factors. First, the behavior of traditional firms responds to economic incentives and market conditions that are politically arranged. Where, for example, labor is cheaper in certain firms, in part it may reflect lower productivity, but usually it also reflects such factors as the lower degree of unionization in smaller companies, the state's willingness to overlook violations of social security, minimum wage, and working conditions' legislation in these firms, and the kind of workers who, despite such conditions, agree to work in these plants. The extent of unionization, the enforcement of industrial legislation, and the availability of a secondary labor force willing to accept bad jobs at bad wages are all facts determined as much by societal and political forces as by economic factors.

Secondly, the traditional sector is shaped by the values, attitudes, and perceptions of it which other groups in society hold and which are translated into rules and objectives for state intervention in the economy. In France and Italy, the one criterion that has above all others shaped conceptions of the traditional firm is that of small, independent, family property. The large firm, no matter how labor intensive or unprofitable or "traditional" in its objectives is not considered traditional, while a dynamic, modern, small shop owned and operated by a single family will, in almost all analyses, political or economic, be lumped together with its traditional small shop neighbors.

These political perceptions receive authoritative expression in organization and legislation. Different institutions and rules have been developed to deal with the traditional and modern sectors of the economy. By this, differences that the simple play of economic forces might have distributed over a continuum are by political decision clustered into distinct and discontinuous segments. A small factory with ten workers may in economic terms be little different from one with twenty employees. But in Italy, where the former one falls into the category of firms which the state defines as artisanal and thus lives in a distinct legal regime established for artisans (with their own banks, tax system, social security rules), the constraints and incentives which the two firms encounter are so diverse that they in fact become quite different.[3] The question raised previously of whether some large firms in France and Italy should be considered part of the traditional sector cannot, therefore, be answered in purely economic terms, for the category is one created by an overlap of economic facts, social perceptions, political values, and state policy.

Despite the heterogeneity in origins and characteristics of the groups that compose it, the traditional sector has a remarkable coherence and unity. This is because the traditional independent classes are, like the working class, political creations. They owe their existence only in part to real, objective similarities in the economic interests of the members of the class but mainly to the members' common perception of having the same situation in society and to society's seeing them as the same and establishing rules that identify them as a political and social entity.[4] As already described for the Italian artisans, public perceptions have in France and Italy been given substance in social and economic legislation and in the structures of interest groups. This political crystallization of interest and value stabilizes the boundaries and membership of the traditional sector. In sum, despite its ambiguities and looseness, the composite definition sketched out does in fact correspond to a relatively stable segment of society.

It follows from this that the groups and firms that belong to the traditional sector vary historically and across societies. It follows also that the notion of the survival of traditional groups does not imply that any given traditional firm or set of firms is old. On the contrary, many of those considered traditional in France and Italy are recent creations. What makes them traditional is not their individual longevity, but rather that they have been established within a particular universe of firms with definite modes of operation and with special relationships to state and society. There is a constant renewal and replacement of those traditional firms that disappear – whether into oblivion or into the modern sector – by other firms operating in similar modes, and the issue of death or survival is better posed as one of the rates of replacement.[5]

The discussion that follows focuses on the industrial and commercial segments of the traditional sector, with only occasional reference to small agriculture. For the purposes of the present argument, the survival in industry and commerce of small firms seems to pose a sharper challenge to our models of industrial societies than does the maintenance of a large number of small cultivators alongside a capitalist agriculture. Moreover, the reasons for the support that small agriculture receives both from large farmers and from the state have been well studied elsewhere, and so will be treated only briefly here in the interest of containing within reasonable limits the material presented in support of our case.[6]

Numbers

In evaluating the numbers in the traditional sectors of France and Italy, we are obliged to settle for estimations of the size and shifts in membership of certain occupational categories and of certain firm categories without being able to compute directly the scale of the traditional sector as a whole. The census categories usually employed offer no basis for systematic distinctions between traditional and modern firms, and, given the political component of our definition, it is hard to imagine any set of socioeconomic categories that would specify completely the dimensions of the traditional sector.[7] As a second-best measure, there are statistics on those groups – small shops, small and medium business, artisans, small agriculture – that do contain virtually all of the traditional sector, though they also include a certain fraction of modern firms that cannot be separated from the others on the basis of the data presented. (In any event, because the operative political distinctions and legislation are usually based on firm size, it is not clear that those modern firms that might be discovered within the size categories that we are treating as traditional ought to be excluded, since their economic behavior, too, is constrained by the fact that they operate under rules established for traditional firms.)

A survey of the size and evolution of those occupational and firm categories in which the mass of the traditional sector is concentrated in France and Italy points to certain conclusions that differ significantly from those suggested by the notion that the traditional sector is on its last legs. First, in terms of numbers alone, traditional firms still represent a sizable mass. There has been an overall decline since World War II of small shops, businesses, and farms, but the numbers that remain are important. Secondly, the general decline masks areas of resilience and expansion. If we examine the thriving parts of the traditional sector, it appears that the critical relationships between traditional firms and the modern sector of the economy, far from eroding and defeating the traditionals, have strengthened them.

To consider first the issue of numbers, while the general phenomenon is decline, what remains of the traditional sector is significant. In France since World War II, the active farm population fell from 20.3 percent of the work force in 1954 to 8.5 percent in 1974. But despite massive rural exodus, the countryside in both France and Italy is still dominated by small and medium family farms. In the same period in which the French active farm population fell to less than half its 1954 level, the proportion of farms under 5 hectares fell only from 35 percent to 31 percent of all farms.[8] In Italy where the agricultural work

Table 1. *Distribution of the French work force employed in industrial plants with over ten employees*[a]

Number of persons in the plant	1906	1926	1931	1936	1954	1962	1966
11–20	12%	10%	10%	10%	8%	8%	8%
21–100	28	28	27	27	28	28	29
101–500	31	30	30	30	31	32	33
500+	29	33	33	33	33	32	30
Totals	100	100	100	100	100	100	100

[a] The 1906 and 1926 figures include all employed in the plant, not only wage earners.
Source: M. Didier and E. Malinvaud, "La concentration de l'industrie s'est-elle accentuée depuis le début du siècle?" *Economie et statistique* (June 1969), p. 7.

force fell by more than half, from 8 million in 1930 to 3.7 million in 1970, the number of farms declined only from 4.2 million to 3.6 million in the same period.[9] At the beginning of the seventies in Italy, the average farm size was well under 10 hectares and half the farms were smaller than 2 hectares.[10]

In commerce in France, the number of small shops has been falling since the fifties: rapidly towards the end of the sixties, then leveling off in the seventies. By 1973, small, independent commerce still represented three-quarters of all French distribution.[11] In Italy, the number of small shops has risen since the war, so that the number of inhabitants per shop, which was 95 in 1951, was only 70 in 1965.[12] For artisans, while the smallest units in France have been in decline, those employing 6 to 9 workers have increased; indeed, in the building trades, the numbers went up by a third in the period 1962–70.[13] As a result, in 1970 artisans still were 10 percent of the active work force in France and in 1972 had a volume of trade three times that of the automobile industry.[14]

In industry, while the tiniest industrial units (plants with fewer than 10 workers) have declined from 39 percent of all plants in 1936 to 25 percent in 1954 and to 20 percent in 1966, there has been remarkable stability in the distribution of plants with over 10 workers (see Table 1).[15] Today's industrial structures in both Italy and France differ sharply from those of the United States in the dimensions of the small-scale sector (see Table 2). If we compare France and Italy, on the one

Table 2. *Industrial plants and work force*

	France (1962)	Italy (1961)	United States (1963)
Average work force			
By plant	11	7	53
By plant of more than 50 persons	215	198	263
By plant of more than 1,000 persons	2,311	2,245	2,580
Work force in median plant[a]	144	64	360
Distribution of work force by plant size. Percentage of personnel employed in plants of –			
More than 1,000	17.3	13.7	30.5
500–999	9.5	7.7	12.4
100–499	27.0	21.6	30.9
50–99	9.8	10.1	9.8
20–49	11.7	11.6	9.1
10–19	5.5	7.3	4.0
5–9	4.6	7.1	2.0
1–4	14.6	20.9	1.3

[a] The median plant is one such that 50% of personnel in the sector are employed in bigger plants and 50% in smaller.
Source: From data in J. P. Nioche et M. Didier, "Deux études sur la dimension des entreprises industrielles," Collections de l'INSEE (El) cited in Bernard Guibert et al., *La Mutation industrielle de la France* (Paris: Collections de l'INSEE, November 1975) nos. E.31, 32, vol. 1., p. 111.

hand, with the United States, on the other, it is striking that the structures of large plants are quite similar (see the average number of persons in plants employing over 50 and over 1,000 persons in Table 2), and that the critical differences are in the space occupied by smaller firms and by the importance within that space of very small firms. Indeed, small firms appear to be growing more rapidly than medium-sized firms and almost as fast as the biggest firms (see Table 3). Shifts in industrial structure, whether measured in terms of plant size or enterprise size, are working to the advantage of medium-small firms rather than medium-large firms or very large firms, and the only real losers are the very tiny enterprises. As the size of the French industrial labor force has remained relatively constant, the proportional distribution of jobs between the traditional and the modern sectors has changed far less than could have been anticipated.[16] In 1975 in

Table 3. *Changes in industrial structure, 1966–70, France*

No. of people employed	No. of firms		Change
	In 1966	In 1970	
0–5	578,170	548,370	−5.15%
6–9	35,950	36,950	+2.71
10–49	55,440	58,610	+5.72
50–199	14,210	14,260	+0.35
200–999	3,830	3,910	+2.09
1,000+	640	680	+6.25

Source: Data from the INSEE 1970 enterprise census (fichier des entreprises de 1970). Cited in CGPME document, "Les Petites et moyennes industries en France en 1970."

France, 97 percent of all industrial firms still employed under 50 workers.[17] In Italy, while the numbers of small and medium firms declined by 14 percent between 1951 and 1969, the population employed in them rose 30 percent, thus increasing the percentage of the industrial work force employed in small and medium firms by 10 percent.[18]

This rapid survey of the numbers in the traditional sectors in France and Italy suggests a magnitude and a resilience far greater than can be easily accounted for as lag. Despite attrition, the structures of the traditional sector have remained remarkably stable; significant groups within it are clearly not candidates for early demise. To save the hypothesis, some have argued that postwar affluence has, by enormously expanding the national pie, made it possible for prosperous societies to pay the price of their less efficient, traditional producers, and thus the process of decline has been slowed, even if not reversed. If this were so, then we would expect the numbers in the traditional sector to fall more rapidly in times of economic crisis, when the resources for satisfying the contradictory claims of modern and traditional producers are diminished. But, in fact, the picture is a mixed one: in times of recession, tight credit, unemployment, and increased competition, major groups in the traditional sector expand. In France in the Great Depression of the thirties, for example, the trend towards decline in the number of tiny industrial plants with fewer than 5 employees, which had been in process since the beginning of the century, suddenly reversed and these firms increased at least until the war.[19] Annie Kriegel has shown how in this period the increase in industrial unemployment gave rise to an increase in small artisanal firms and in the numbers employed in them.[20] Those expelled from industry set up small workshops on their own; wives sought employment to supplement their husbands' declining industrial incomes.

In Italy over the past decade, the massive decentralization of industrial production that began in response to increased labor rigidities in large plants has been accelerated by the economic crisis. For example, a study of the metalworking industry in Bologna province showed that between 1971 and 1975 the proportion of firms employing over 100 workers that subcontracted out work rose from 80 percent to 98 percent; at the same time, the number of tiny firms employing fewer than 20 workers grew rapidly and the rate of expansion of employment in these artisanal firms was higher than in any other firm size category.[21] In efforts to explain why Italy seemed so prosperous at a time when all the official economic indicators suggested stagnation and massive unemployment, economists began to estimate the "hidden" production and employment of the traditional sector.[22] They discovered through sample surveys that actual rates of participation in the work force were as much as twice the official rates and that in 1978, for example, the actual rate of growth of industrial production, officially reported as 2.5 percent, was more likely to have been between 5 percent and 7 percent.[23] The differences between the actual and the reported measures of production and employment are virtually all attributable to activity in small and medium firms. While it is too soon to be able to study systematically the impact of the economic crisis of the mid-seventies on the traditional sectors of France and Italy, the general picture that emerges from a variety of evidence is one of considerable resilience and even expansion.

The uses of the traditional sector

The strength of traditional firms, most strikingly, even in times of economic crisis, suggests that their presence in advanced industrial societies cannot be understood simply as the product of lag or as a residual. Rather, as we will argue, the vitality of the traditional sector in France and Italy results from functions that traditional groups perform for the modern sector and can be analyzed in the web of relations that link traditional firms to the operation and evolution of the economic system and the political system.

The availability of traditional groups makes it likely that certain problems common to industrial societies will be solved by resort to the traditional sector, and for these purposes, traditional groups may be protected, reinforced, or recreated. When traditional groups are not present in significant numbers, as they are not in the United States, other, functionally equivalent solutions to these problems must be found. Before considering the functions performed for the modern sector by traditional groups, several observations are necessary.

First, even where traditional groups are extremely useful to modern firms and to the state, their existence cannot be accounted for by the needs they serve. Traditional groups have their origins in social, economic, and political systems altogether different from those in which they operate today, and their structures and capabilities are strongly marked and constrained by their histories[24] *The modern sector exploits a network of traditional firms it finds already in place.* Where this network is still substantial, as in Italy, it can be reinforced and expanded for new purposes. But traditional firms cannot be created *de novo* in industrial societies and, indeed, where they have declined too far, they cannot be resurrected. In Italy, for example, in the seventies, the economic problems created by high labor costs and inflexible labor supply could be dealt with by a massive increase in subcontracting to artisanal firms and by an expansion of home labor and of the putting-out system, because these traditional structures had remained quite important even through the heyday of the economic miracle. Though France in the same period experienced the same labor difficulties, the virtual disappearance of these traditional structures made it impossible to move work out of factories, and the French had to resort to altogether different solutions to the same problem. (See Piore in this volume.)

Secondly, though the groups' role in contemporary societies cannot be deduced from their origins, without their histories, we cannot explain the characteristics of the solutions they provide. Considered as one of a set of functional alternatives to certain problems of industrialism, the traditional sector carries baggage from the past along with it into the resolution of these problems. Thus, when the problem of rigidities in the labor market are dealt with in Italy by the decentralization of production and in the United States by the employment of blacks and aliens, the outcomes differ in ways that can only be accounted for by the history of traditionalism in Italy and of racism in the United States.

Finally, understanding the specific historical processes through which different groups come to carry out parallel roles in various societies is the more important because, when considered closely, the problems that seem common to all industrial societies turn out to be significantly different according to how they arose, were perceived, and were resolved. To return to the same example, American and Italian industry do in one sense confront the same problem of increasingly rigid labor supply. But however identical the terms of the problem are in a technical sense, the terms in which politicians, businessmen, and trade unionists see the issue, the resources available to them for solving it, and the range of policies acceptable to the public are so shaped by the different ways in which the issue has emerged historically that the problem can hardly be considered the same in the two societies. Looked at in this light, the chance that solutions can be successfully exported to other countries with the "same problem" is slight. Without major political disruptions or radical shifts in the structure of social and economic incentives, Italians are no more likely to be able to accept the firing of workers as a way of increasing productivity and reducing labor costs than Americans are able to create traditional, small firms and shift labor into them as ways of achieving the same ends.

In sum, it is not possible for us to pursue the analysis of the role of traditional groups in industrial societies very far without specifying the history of the actors, the action, and the national context, or else fall into circular arguments about survival and functionality. Traditional groups survive because they are used for purposes essential to the stability of modern societies; but the meaning of stability and its prerequisites in different societies vary precisely because of the absence or presence of a traditional sector.

Economic uses of traditional firms

To ground an analysis of the role of traditional firms in advanced industrial economies, we should be able to show why the structures of production, of the labor force, and of demand generate tensions and roadblocks for which remedy must be sought outside the mechanisms that regulate the economy in its normal mode. To do this, Michael Piore has argued, the neoclassical theory of the normal pattern of operation of capitalist economies must be called into question. The model in which the motivations of economic actors and the structures of production are conceptualized as reflecting a single mode of rational, maximizing behavior would have to be replaced with a model with differentiated and discontinuous behaviors and structures. Piore has suggested the assumptions about economic behavior on which a model might be constructed that would incorporate the relationships between primary and secondary sectors, or modern and traditional sectors, into the central explanation, instead of leaving them in the penumbra of transitional and marginal phenomena. Here we intend only to deal with the narrower issue of the economic services the traditional sector renders, and in this way to describe the advantages modern industrial economies enjoy because of the presence of traditional groups and the apparent sacrifices that modern firms make in order to maintain them.

In France and Italy, the traditional sector has performed three major functions for the economy. First, it continues to provide a range of products that consumers desire but that modern firms do not produce. These products usually require artisanal production or personalized services. While the demand for such goods has generally declined, affluence has generated a certain new demand for goods that are not mass produced. Moreover, as Annie Kriegel has pointed out in a study of artisans in a Paris district, small producers often do well in times of crisis and war because they are able to provide products and services that larger firms are not able or are no longer able to make.[25] During World War II, for example, the Paris artisans Kriegel studied did repairs on objects that in prosperous times would have been discarded for new ones, improvised replacement parts, built machines that would function with available fuels, and fixed radios to receive broadcasts from London!

Secondly, the traditional sector has kept a significant fraction of the work force employed in firms of a kind that discourage labor militance and organization and generally offer lower wages and poorer working conditions. As Piore points out in Chapter 2, the events of May–June 1968 in France, and of the fall of 1969 in Italy, pushed large employers to cast about for ways of reducing the increased labor costs in their own plants. Transferring work to smaller firms offered this possibility. There is abundant evidence for both France and Italy of the wage differential between small and large firms. Studies in France of the lowest paid workers have found them disproportionately clustered in firms with fewer than 50 employees.[26] For lack of systematic data, it is more difficult to demonstrate that in France jobs carried out in small firms earn lower wages than identical jobs performed for big firms.[27] What evidence there is comes from scattered data on wages in subcontractors and from interviews with employers and Ministry of Industry officials on the factors that promote subcontracting. These sources suggest that the lower wages in the smaller, owner-run firms are often decisive in terms of survival for the firm.[28]

In Italy, in contrast, the picture is far clearer, for in response to the phenomenon of a great increase in the quantity of work shifted out of large, modern firms into smaller, more traditional ones, research on wages, working conditions, and unionization in firms of different dimensions has flourished. Wages are lower in smaller firms in every industrial branch (see Table 4), and industry case studies show that essentially identical work in small and large firms earns very different wages and social benefits.[29] For example, a study of wages in small

Table 4. Hourly wages (in thousands of lira), Italy, third trimester 1974, Firms by size

Industrial branch	10–49 workers		50–90 workers		100–99 workers		200–499 workers		500–999 workers		1,000+ workers		Total workers	
	Direct salary[a]	Compre-hensive salary[b]	Direct salary	Compre-hensive salary	Direct salary	Compre-hensive salary	Direct salary	Compre-hensive salary	Direct salary	Compre-hensive salary	Direct salary	Compre-hensive salary	Direct salary	Compre-hensive salary
Extractive	1.149	1.471	1.272	1.657	1.473	2.044	1.577	2.265	1.594	2.187	1.504	2.062	1.382	1.867
Food	1.046	1.402	1.153	1.529	1.233	1.627	1.280	1.635	1.380	1.863	1.354	1.885	1.222	1.620
Textile and garment	0.942	1.337	1.042	1.466	1.085	1.578	1.177	1.703	1.218	1.753	1.243	1.934	1.106	1.598
Metalworking and transportation	1.060	1.459	1.175	1.636	1.238	1.753	1.329	1.908	1.381	2.054	1.446	2.131	1.323	1.914
Chemical	1.171	1.589	1.318	1.823	1.438	1.968	1.499	2.071	1.641	2.170	1.693	2.121	1.562	2.047
Miscellaneous	0.942	1.272	1.055	1.431	1.148	1.568	1.276	1.764	1.394	1.959	1.527	2.307	1.159	1.605
Construction	1.096	1.441	1.178	1.536	1.243	1.637	1.379	1.812	1.413	1.936	1.424	1.825	1.172	1.542
Electricity and gas	1.626	2.005	1.834	2.321	1.823	2.393	2.003	2.704	1.729	2.191	1.779	2.439	1.779	2.410
Total	1.024	1.381	1.127	1.533	1.203	1.662	1.307	1.822	1.400	1.996	1.501	2.162	1.261	1.761

[a]Direct earnings include: wages paid on an hourly or other basis; piecework; special rates for overtime, holiday, and night work; incentives and special indemnities; an evaluation of payments in kind (e.g., cafeteria) and corresponding compensatory indemnities.
[b]Total earnings include: holiday and vacation pay; gratuities; family payments; other salary supplements.
Source: Ministero del Lavoro e della Previdenza Sociale, Direzione generale del collocamento della Manodopera, Divisione VII, "Indagini statistiche dell' impiego."

printing firms compared with wages at a big publishing company (Mondadori) shows that wages in the former ranged from 43 percent to 70 percent of those at the latter for similar work.[30] In industries where work can be put out to home workers, the differentials between the cost of labor for work in the factory and work outside are enormous, as a study of the costs of home workers as compared with factory workers in the Modena stocking industry showed: 588 lira per hour compared with 854 lira.[31] These studies demonstrate that working conditions as well as wages are worse in smaller firms and that, with some exceptions, workers are less organized than in larger firms. The workers are not only not unionized – they are not even officially registered as employed. Various local studies show that where the official statistics report only 30 percent to 40 percent employment, door-to-door checks find 50 percent to 70 percent employed.[32] The underreporting of employment reflects the employers' interest in hiding from the government the numbers they employ, in order to evade paying into social security funds. It is hardly surprising that these "illegal" workers are unorganized and that the unions are only beginning to make inroads in this population. In France, too, small firms are less unionized.

The existence of a reservoir of more docile workers may have a dampening effect on labor agitation and on wage increases throughout the entire economy. It is possible to make the opposite argument as well: that the existence of this "exploited" sector makes possible the high wages of the modern sector. This point of view has been developed by Vera Lutz, George Hildebrand, and most recently by Giorgio Fuà.[33] In this perspective, both the employers and the workers in the modern sector have a stake in the preservation of the traditional firms. At the very least, however, the vitality of this network of traditional firms provides employers with the opportunity of shifting work out of highly unionized, highly politicized plants with well-paid workers and large bills for social security into productive units with lower costs and fewer constraints on managerial decisions. Even though all work cannot be transferred, still, as the Italian example since 1969 demonstrates, much more can be transferred than anyone imagined or predicted. And whatever advantage the workers in big plants derive from the system, it can hardly be regarded as permanent as long as the quota of work in the big plants is being reduced.

The third function that the traditional sector performs is to contribute flexibility to economies that have become increasingly more rigid because of the magnitude of capital investment and the power of trade-union organization. The relative ease with which the traditional sector expands and contracts and its greater sensitivity to the economic cycle all help compensate for a loss of responsiveness in the system as a whole. The flexibility that the traditional sector provides to the economy results from particular kinds of producers, particular kinds of firms, and the relationships that these workers and firms enter into with the modern sector. To begin with the producers, the traditional firm harbors three types: the independent, self-employed entrepreneur; the worker excluded, permanently or temporarily, from employment in the modern sector; and the workers whose wages and conditions of work are substantially equivalent to those of comparable workers in modern firms. The first two categories are those that provide the flexibility in the system, and were they to decline in proportion to the third type, the distinctive advantages of traditional firms would also disappear.

The behavior of independent entrepreneurs of the traditional sector differs significantly from the industrialists and managers of the modern sector, not only because of the structures in which they operate but also because of the values and objectives they pursue. Family owned and run businesses exhibit a pattern of behavior different from firms in the modern sector that are typically run by managers. Dean Savage concludes in his study of French business that these differences result over time in higher growth for manager-run firms and the perpetuation of the owner-run firms in the lower levels of the firm size hierarchy.[34] It is not size as such that determines growth, but rather the greater or lesser likelihood that firms of given sizes will be run by family members (heirs and the like) or by professional managers. The result, in the case of the former, is a management style less conducive to expansion.

Among the differences that distinguish the owners of the traditional sector, one relevant to explaining the flexibility that these producers contribute to the economy is the extent to which decisions are based on social and familial factors instead of narrowly economic ones. Savage has analyzed one reason for this: The managers of small firms are very often its owners and likely to be contemplating its eventual passage into the hands of their children. Another is that small firms are tied to a single locality, where the owner's reputation and influence are at stake in his business behavior. He uses his firm not only to maximize economic return but also to build social prestige.

The heavier weight of social considerations in the economic behavior of small, independent producers leads to significant differences in the ways they use labor and capital, thus accounting in part for the flexibility these firms provide the economy. First, as employers, the independent, small owners are likely to absorb more labor than their firm requires and in particular to acknowledge the claims of family members to employment in the family enterprise. In hard times, shops, farms, and small industry open their doors to let in family members that have lost jobs elsewhere. Next, given the owner's close involvement in his business, its small size, and its entwinement with family, relationships between employers and workers are often cast in a paternalistic mode, whether benevolent or authoritarian. The pattern of labor relations that develops in small, traditional firms discourages workers' organization and supports personalized links between employers and employees. The owners' attitudes and presence are thus important determinants, though not the only ones, of the low degree of unionization of traditional firms.

Finally, the intermeshing of the fortunes of firm and family makes small independents less likely to invest any funds other than those generated by the business. While their first concern may be risk, probably as important are the dangers of state interference that arise whenever investment requires outside financing. Given widespread practices of tax evasion and underpayment into social security funds in small firms in both France and Italy, there is much to fear from letting the state into the family books. On broader grounds, there is an aversion to letting outsiders into family business. The consequence of these attitudes is a preference for more labor-intensive technologies over those requiring investment in capital equipment. In sum, the values and social situation of the small independents, whether shopkeepers, small and medium businessmen, farmers, or artisans, predispose them to operate in ways that make it possible to absorb or get rid of labor easily. It is precisely this possibility that is less and less available to firms in the modern sector, where the rigidities introduced by unionization and by massive capital investment have made it increasingly more difficult to respond to cyclical changes.

On the side of the workers, preferences and vulnerabilities account for their acceptance of the insecurity and lower wages of the traditional firms. The traditional sector employs a disproportionate number of women, very young and very old men, and peasants with farms they still work. These disparate categories have in common, first, that they are regarded as inferior labor by the employers in the modern sector and, hence, in all but boom times have a weak position in the labor market. Secondly, most of these workers have shelters from which they derive supplemental income and to which they can return if unemployed: The home and the income of other family members is usually available to women and the young and the old; peasants and migrant workers can return to the farm. These shelters make it possible for groups with weaker labor market positions to survive; they may also account for a greater willingness to accept such employment. In some cases, these groups may prefer jobs in and out of which they can move easily – the young experimenting before settling into a permanent position, women while bringing up children, peasants still working their land. This last factor should not be overemphasized, since there is considerable evidence that when better paying, more stable jobs are available, workers in the traditional sector take them.[35] In fact, in Italy a growing part of the work force in small enterprises has at some point been able to work in large plants and has subsequently been expelled from them, so the issue is not that of the incapacity of the labor force of the traditional sector for work in modern firms, but rather of their aptitude and availability for work in traditional firms.[36]

Managers and workers in the traditional sector, then, have social situations, resources, and predispositions that make them appropriate for and willing to assume particular kinds of work and entrepreneurship. There is no reason to believe that many of these groups might not function as well if placed, with appropriate training, into jobs in modern firms. The social characteristics of the producers of the traditional sector do not determine their work roles, let alone account for the persistence of traditional enterprises. Rather, these characteristics should be seen as a necessary condition for the operation of traditional firms whose survival and even expansion depend on particular relationships with the modern sector. Without such workers and entrepreneurs, it would be impossible to maintain traditional firms; but even with them, the traditional sector would disappear unless it received support, protection, and new life from its links to the modern economy.

The central mechanism through which modern firms exploit the advantages of flexibility and lower labor costs of the small, traditional firms is the transfer to them of work out of large plants with heavy capital investment, advanced technology, high labor costs, and inflexible labor supply. What kinds of work and how much work have been transferred out of the modern sector into traditional firms has varied between the two countries and has changed over time. In both countries, some subcontracting arrangements between modern and traditional firms reflect the relative advantages of scale and technology that make production of particular goods in firms of different sizes more or less profitable. But subcontracting based on specialization – which is the dominant type in the United States – is far less important in France and Italy than subcontracting of a conjunctural type.[37] In order to avoid hiring workers whom it will be next to impossible to fire if demand falls and to produce more without making major investments in plant and equipment, modern firms often respond to increased demand by increasing the amount of work that is subcontracted. For example, many of the same parts that are being produced in the Fiat Company are also being produced by small firms that are Fiat subcontractors; in good times, the volume of work that Fiat shifts into the subcontracting firms increases; in bad times, a higher quota of work is performed within the big enterprise. In contrast, subcontracting in the American automobile industry is based on specialization, and a different array of products from those being manufactured in the "mother company" are turned out by subcontractors.

In France and Italy, subcontracting is used mainly as a way of shifting the burden of economic risk and uncertainty that derives from fluctuations in demand. The interest of the large modern firms lies not in integrating traditional firms but rather in preserving their autonomy, for despite technological backwardness, lower productivity, and even sometimes the inferior quality of their output, they still provide an essential flexibility. How valuable this flexibility is to the modern firms has been underscored by developments over the past few years in Italy, where despite the economic crisis, the quota of work subcontracted out of big plants has risen, not fallen. This means that big plants are willing to leave capital equipment underutilized in order to avoid hiring, since hiring means increasing the constraints on managerial decision as well as increasing labor costs: both problems that can be minimized by shifting work instead to small subcontracting firms.

Some of these economic relationships between the traditional and modern sectors provide benefits that accrue to the system as a whole and not to particular firms. As pointed out earlier, one such advantage might be that wage demands are restrained by the presence in traditional firms of a large supply of workers receiving wages lower than those of the modern firms. Another service that the traditional sector renders the economy as a whole is to reduce unemployment. In Italy, the major increases in employment in the postwar period have been in jobs in small and small-medium firms and not in the large-scale, modern sector. Given the apparent incapacity of the latter to create a significant number of new jobs, the traditional sector clearly has played a critical role in keeping the numbers of the unemployed and of those forced to migrate abroad at a tolerable level. Small shops and small agriculture, too, are sponges that absorb the workers that the modern economy cannot employ. For this reason, commerce in Italy has been described as a "refuge activity," as "a safety valve for unemployment that has led politicians to swallow the idea of a commercial class which, because made up of family units, deserves to be protected and defended."[38] Agriculture in Italy in the years of the economic crisis has taken back many of those who left the farm for industrial employment: In recent years, as many workers may have returned South as those who left it for Northern employment. Maggioli concluded from a study of the small agricultural sector of the highly industrialized province of Lombardy that, despite the small numbers involved, the little farm "still functions as a shock-absorbing element in the recurrent economic and employment crises of our region."[39]

It is not only the absolute numbers employed in the traditional sector that are critical for the stability of the economic system but also the traditional sector's capacity to expand or contract its labor force, in times of recession to absorb workers expelled from the modern sector, in times of growth to provide workers for the modern sector. The elasticity of the traditional firms make them the shock absorbers of the economy. So when the road ahead looks bumpy, the attention of the Italian political elites is rapidly focused on that part of the economic machine that has in the past protected the engine from shocks that might have destroyed it; that is, they revert to protection of the traditional firms.

In France, too, the linkages between solutions to the unemployment problem and the presence of the traditional sector have become increasingly visible during the recent economic crisis. In contrast to Italy, France in postwar years suffered from labor shortages, not surpluses, and so the traditional sector was seen as bottling up unproductive labor that ought to be released for work in modern firms. The major constraint on policies that shrank the traditional sector was concern about the political reactions of the workers who were to be thus "liberated" from their unproductive activities. Only in the past few years, as unemployment climbed to its highest levels since the Depression, has there been a growing recognition of the possibilities of maintaining and promoting employment by supporting traditional firms.

The political uses of the traditional sector

The issue of employment brings into play not only the economic but also the political functions of the traditional sector, for what is at stake is political stability and not simply the productive and profitable functioning of the economy. In the narrowest sense, the political importance of the traditional sector can be calculated by its numbers and its electorate which, though declining, are still substantial in both France and Italy. In France, the number of votes controlled by small, independent property holders and their families falls between 3 and 4 million; for Italy in 1968, Sylos-Labini estimated 9.3 million electors in this category.[40] And yet, numbers understate the importance of the traditional sector; for aside from the weight of its electors, it plays a vital role in preserving political and social order. Throughout the postwar period, the grand schemes for industrialization and modernization of economy and society never entirely supplanted a second set of policies that were pursued to protect the small firms that the first set of policies were designed to eliminate. In part, these contradictions can be explained by the economic uses of the traditional sector for modern enterprises that have already been described. But the protection of the traditional sector also reflects the political elite's recognition of the specifically political uses of small, independent property. First, this sector protects society from unrest and explosions by the obstacles it puts in the way of a radical mobilization of the working class. Next, because the traditional middle classes themselves are important elements in the political consensus underpinning the regime in the two countries, their disaffection can have major destabilizing consequences. Finally, groups with an economic and social base in the traditional economy are pivotal in the political alliances on which the governing parties in both countries depend.

Demobilization of the working class

The traditional sector's resources for solving problems which might otherwise lead to a radicalization of other social groups are nowhere more important or obvious than in the area of employment. In France and Italy, unemployment is believed to have the potential for creating serious political unrest. As one official in Confindustria, the Italian national business confederation, expressed it, "More or less unemployment equals more or less social tension." With rising levels of unemployment over the past years, the French and Italian governments have cast about for new solutions, however temporary, for the labor surplus. Higher compensation for the unemployed, financial incentives to industry to keep workers on at least part time (*chômage partiel*), state funds to pay the wages of young workers who would be otherwise without jobs, loans, tax credits, and aid to keep dying industries alive awhile longer – these and other schemes currently being tried in France and Italy were all devised to stave off the mass discontent that is feared to result from high levels of unemployment.

In this overall strategy, small firms of the traditional sector play a critical part, for they absorb far more labor than large, modern firms. In Italy, the shortage of work has been a problem throughout the postwar period, and the regime constantly has had to worry about the political mobilization by the Right or the Left of workers with no jobs or insecure employment. While the planners and the high rhetoric of the parties called for modernization of the economy, the actual policies adopted protected small shops against supermarkets, sheltered small businesses from the full impact of social security and fiscal legislation, and doled out subsidies and exemptions to the very traditional firms whose existence blocked the expansion of the modern sector. These contradictions are best understood as the price that had to be paid by the modern capitalist sector for maintaining what Alessandro Pizzorno has described as "a strategy of alliance with the small, productive bourgeoisie in the task of controlling social tension." As Pizzorno explains,

By providing solutions of political protection to the problem of precarious work, a solidarity was created between the small employer and the worker, since they were both dependent on a certain policy and not on the market. The complicity was shared. On one hand, the government had an interest in seeing that stability was not disturbed, and therefore in a calculated fashion granted its protection; on the other hand, the small bourgeoisie could blackmail the government, since the latter had to help it in order to avoid the explosive situations that could result from the extreme distress of precarious workers. Out of this arose a *de facto* alliance between the small bourgeoisie and marginal social strata, and a complicity of all in a policy of protection of precarious work.[41]

Traditional firms ward off social unrest not only by providing work but by placing it in a setting in which organization and mobilization of labor are extremely difficult. The dispersion of the work force in small, productive units, the personalized relations between worker and employer in these small units, and the characteristics of the work force all reduce the chances for mass action in traditional firms.

Finally, the traditional sector provides a channel of individual success that drains social frustrations that might otherwise flow into collective action and directs them towards individual projects for obtaining access to the class of small property holders. The demobilizing dream of moving out of the factory and out of the working class survives best when enough small stores, artisanal shops, and little businesses remain as alternative poles of attraction for the potential recruits of radical class action.[42] In France, these last considerations – the weakness of political and syndical organization in traditional firms, the attractive pull of small property as a force to counteract the pulls toward collective action – have historically been more important than the labor absorptive capacity of the traditional sector.

Middle-class protest

Supporting the traditional sector is perceived as critical in France and Italy, not only to block mobilization of the working class, but also to prevent radicalization of the middle classes that earn a living from small property. In Italy, the belief that a revolt of the small, propertied middle class explains historic fascism and contemporary protofascist movements has united the parties of government and those of the left opposition around policies to win over, or at least to neutralize, the traditional sector. The *qualunquismo* of the early postwar period, the growth of the neo-Fascist party (*Movimento sociale italiano*), periodic outbursts of urban violence like the Reggio Calabria revolt, and the left- and right-wing *squadrismo* of the last decade (the red brigades, the nappisti, etc.) all derive substantial support from groups whose social base is small, independent property.

For the Christian Democrats and the smaller parties of the government majorities of the postwar period, these movements threaten to take away part of their electorate. Sylos-Labini has estimated that small, independent propertied groups, which constitute 31 percent of the Italian population, make up 36 percent of the Democrazia cristiana (DC) electorate and 42 percent of the electorates of the DC's frequent allies, the Republicans and the Liberals.[43] Even more important in Christian Democratic concerns – given the relative stability of the electorate until the seventies – is the fear of social breakdown and anarchy, for over and over again the state has demonstrated that it is impotent to halt civil violence. Governments of the postwar period have raced to stay ahead of their competition on the Right in order to prevent the mobilization of the traditional electorate. At each moment of political stirrings in that quarter, the government has responded with a flow of subsidies, laws, and special treatment for small property.

The Communists and Socialists, with twenty years in political exile reflecting on the causes of fascism behind them, regard the mobilization of the middle classes as a danger to democracy and as one of the principal threats to Left prospects in Italy. It would be impossible to understand the alacrity with which the Partito comunista italiano (PCI) absorbed the "lessons of Chile" without realizing the extent to which the party's entire postwar experience – its organizational structures, behavior in local, regional, and parliamentary institutions, strategies for coming to power, – has been shaped by the "lessons of fascism." Chief of these lessons is the need to neutralize, if not win over, the middle classes, whose hostility to democracy and, even more, to socialism, makes them willing allies of reactionary political forces. The Left therefore vies with the Christian Democrats in presenting itself as the protector of small, independent property and has gone along with most of the protectionist legislation of the postwar period.[44] The Communists, for example, voted for the 1972 Helfer law that regulated the opening of new supermarkets and virtually halted the modernization of commerce. While railing against the high cost of living, the PCI called for rapid implementation of this legislation "in order to block the expansion of monopolistic supermarkets and the proliferation of licenses."[45]

In the cities and regions its elected officials govern, the Communist Party has made special efforts to reassure the small, propertied middle class. One important objective of the "Bologna model of socialism" has been to demonstrate to shopkeepers and businessmen in small and medium-sized firms that their interests are better served, or at least not endangered, by Communists in government. Despite the relative success in these areas in reducing hostility of the middle class, the reactions of these groups in the event of Communist participation in government remains a major preoccupation of the party. The *compromesso storico*, like its lineal ancestor, the *via italiana al socialismo*, is a strategy for bringing the Communists into national government without provoking an uncontrollable and violent response from segments of the middle class. The *compromesso storico*, by associating the PCI with the DC in government, would provide a shield against United States and European reactions; at the same time, by using the DC to control its traditional electors, the most dangerous sources of domestic opposition would be held in leash.

In France, the radicalization of the small, propertied middle class in the postwar period has produced one major explosion, the Poujadist movement (UDCA), and several bombs of lesser impact: Gérard Nicoud and the CID-UNATI, Jean Royer, UNICER.[46] In contrast to Italy, where fascism directed the violence of the traditional middle classes against the Left, the mobilization of the same groups in France has been aimed against the state.[47] As Stanley Hoffmann put it, in discussing why the Poujadist movement started as an attack against taxes: "It is a law of French political life that the revolts of the middle classes against proletarianization take the form of an insurrection against the State."[48] The major movements of the French middle classes in the postwar period have had as their main targets government, the administration, and – because the state has been monopolized for the past twenty years by the Gaullists and minor allies – the Center-Right. Though anticommunism, anticollectivism, and antirepublicanism are present in some measure in all of the movements, these themes are secondary to the attack on the rulers.

The most striking case is the Poujade movement, since it came at a point when the strength of the Socialist and Communist Parties and the Cold War might well have turned it against the Left.[49] Poujadism grew out of a 1953 tax revolt by shopkeepers and artisans in central France, spread to other social categories, and climaxed in the 1956 election with 2.5 million votes for Poujadist lists and 52 Poujadist deputies. As Hoffmann points out, Poujadism grew out of precisely those social milieux that had historically supported the Republic. Unlike the Right of the Third Republic or Vichy, Poujade's targets were not the regime and its institutions but, rather, their perversion and corruption by technocrats and big business. When Poujade did attack the Left, it was for the same reasons that he scourged the groups representing modern capitalist interests: that it destroyed the initiative, personality, and freedoms of the individual. But the anticommunism of the movement was so secondary a theme in the early heroic days, that Poujade proudly displayed a Communist in the leadership group, and Communists played an important role in the UDCA in several departments.

In the Fifth as in the Fourth Republic, protest movements of the traditional middle class have been destabilizing, not because they threaten the balance of Left-Right forces, but because they attack the government. After a decade of quiescence, violent protest from the traditional sector revived in 1969 with a mobilization of shopkeepers and artisans under the banner of organizations known as the CID-UNATI and the leadership of Gérard Nicoud.[50] Nicoud, like Poujade before him, laid the troubles of small, independent property at the doorstep of the technocrats and big-business interests in government and declared that the only effective resistance was a frontal attack on the state.

Why were we forced to illegality? Of all the French social classes, we were the only one that until 1969 had expressed its discontent with only pious wishes or legal protest. The result as of January 1, 1969: NOTHING, absolutely NOTHING. . . . May 1968 was to reveal to us the path we had to take. Not only did the government, though well aware of our serious problems, do nothing for us, but, terrified by the wave that threatened to carry it away, it leaned on us for support; flattering us, invoking "the flag," the "Republic,". . . . What a disillusion! All we got were more supermarkets. . . .

No one can deny the evidence if they compare what our social class obtained up to 1969 with the results since 1969 [i.e., since CID-UNATI violence],. . . . Whose fault is it that *concertation* takes place in the street? Above all, the Executive's.[51]

After four years of mass rallies, attacks on tax offices, kidnappings of tax inspectors, and CID-UNATI victories in the elections for Chambers of Commerce, the government yielded major concessions to the traditional sector. The Parliament passed a bill regulating commercial development that protected traditional commerce against supermarkets by creating departmental commissions to rule on any new stores over certain dimensions.[52] In these commissions were equal numbers of local elected officials and representatives of shopkeepers and artisans; and the results of their deliberations were predictably unfavorable to new commercial development: 30 percent fewer supermarket openings in the year after the passage of the law.[53] In 1975, the tax system was reformed, and the *patente* replaced with a professional tax. In the first year of the new system, artisans paid 53 percent less than they would have with the old tax; shopkeepers with fewer than three employees paid 62 percent less than with the *patente*. For 29 percent of the artisans and 39 percent of the shopkeepers, the new tax was less than 25 percent of the *patente*![54] These concessions to traditional middle-class groups did more than run counter to the interests of powerful groups in the modern sector whose growth was constrained, as in the case of supermarkets, or those who were required to bear a heavier tax load. The effect of these concessions (as the then Minister of Finance, Giscard d'Estaing, who opposed the new law on commerce, had predicted) was to contribute to inflation, which would become the government's principal concern.

In both France and Italy, then, the mobilization of discontent in the traditional sector remains a major preoccupation of government. Even when the interests of major capitalist groups must be sacrificed or when vital objectives, like keeping prices down, are at stake, important concessions are made to quell unrest in the class of small, independent property holders. For the parties in opposition, the situation is, however, quite different in the two countries, with the Italian Communists devoting considerable resources to programs for the traditional middle class, in order to avert a potentially disruptive middle-class reaction to a Left government. In France, the fact that traditional middle-class protest has focused on the state and not on the Left has rendered the opposition parties far less sensitive than the Italians to the problems that might arise from the resistance and hostility of small, independent property holders were the Left to form a government.[55]

Parties, alliances, and elections

As the traditional electorate shrank in the postwar period, its weight in the strategies and alliances of political parties might have been expected to diminish in parallel. In fact, the importance of the traditional sector for the parties of government in France and Italy seems to have remained relatively stable, perhaps to have increased over the past decade; while for the parties in opposition, now nearer to power than ever before, the effort to neutralize, if not win over, the traditional electorate has acquired new urgency.

In both France and Italy, three long-term political processes have been at work to maintain and increase the importance of the traditional electorate, despite its declining numbers. First, the "catch-all" parties of government – the Christian Democrats in Italy, the Gaullists in France – are experiencing changes in their social bases of support. The working class and even salaried middle-class supporters are falling away, leaving these parties dependent on an alliance of the most advanced and the most backward groups: of elites at the top of the modern capitalist economy and of the traditional sector. Secondly, in both countries, the competition between Left and Right has become closer. The major Center-Right parties are maintaining their positions by pulling electors from the small, centrist parties; the Left has gained in strength by winning a higher proportion of new electors and by attracting some defectors from the Center-Right. Finally, the relations between the dominant party of the majority and its habitual allies have become more competitive. Where once the parties of governmental coalitions in both countries had relatively fixed and agreed-upon "shares of the market," now the largest party of the Center-Right is attempting to absorb its allies' electors.

The first and perhaps most important of the shifts of the past decade with this effect has been the gradual transformation of the social bases of the principal parties of government. The Christian Democrats in Italy, the Gaullists in France have been described as "catchall people's parties," appealing to the whole population for votes, unlike class-based parties which attempt to mobilize particular segments of the electorate.[56] These parties present themselves as "interclassist" and, in fact, until the late sixties, both drew substantial support from all classes. The composition of their electorates closely matched the socioeconomic composition of the population. The most revealing measure of the interclassist nature of these Center-Right parties was their success in winning working-class votes. In France, through the first decade of the Fifth Republic, one-third of the blue-collar working class voted Gaullist.[57] For Italy, Sylos-Labini has estimated that 35 percent of the working class voted for the DC in 1968.[58]

The emergence of the catchall people's party was interpreted as part of a larger phenomenon, the modernization of European politics, with the disappearance of ideological parties and the rise of parties with pragmatic, broad-based appeals to the electorate. Though the function of ideology in enlarging or limiting the electorate of the catchall parties was not altogether neglected in the theory of the catchall party, it was considered as distinctly secondary.[59] In retrospect, however, the nationalism personified in General de Gaulle, the Catholicism represented in the organizations, traditions, and values of the DC appear to have been far more potent elements in the construction of catchall party coalitions than was recognized. In France, after de Gaulle's departure from power, the electorate of the Union démocratique républicaine (UDR) began to narrow. Blue-collar workers, who had constituted 27 percent of the Gaullist electorate in 1965, were 22 percent of the majority electorate in 1973 and 17 percent in 1976.[60] Middle-level "cadres" and employees, who were 20 percent of the Union pour la nouvelle république (UNR) electorate in 1965, were 16 percent of the majority electorate in 1973 and 14 percent in 1976. Over the same period, the traditional groups in society came to constitute a more significant part of the majority's electors: Farmers were 13 percent of the UNR electorate in 1965, 13 percent of the majority electorate in 1973, and 24 percent in 1976. Retired persons and those without profession, who had been 24 percent of the Gaullist electorate in 1965, were 30 percent of the majority's in 1976.

In Italy, the interclassist appeal of the DC was inextricably connected to the strength of Catholic values, traditions, and organizations incorporated in a subculture whose members were loyal DC electors. With the erosion of the Catholic subculture, the spillover from religious practice to political choice has been reduced. Electors who once felt bound by religious conviction to vote for the DC are now freed to shift their ballots.[61] The party's reduced leverage on practicing Catholics increases the probabilities not only of loss of the DC's working-class electors but also of women and youth.[62] The effects of the weakening of the Catholic supports of the catchall party have only begun to appear in electoral behavior. Until the seventies, the Italian electorate was remarkably stable, despite generational turnover and geographical mobility. Even in 1976, the Communists' great electoral leap forward did not so much draw on defectors from the Center-Right as on electors casting ballots for the first time and on transfers of votes from other Left parties.[63] In Italy today, the decrease in the interclassist appeal of the DC is still at an early stage, and the DC still draws substantial support from all segments of the population. Nonetheless, with the withering away of the links that tied the Catholic electors to the party, the same set of changes appear to be in progress in the DC as in the Gaullist party, with the same results: a decline in the working-class, white-collar, and urban electorate. As Parisi and Pasquino commented on the 1976 legislative elections:

Perhaps the most worrisome aspect of the June 20 election was the likely concentration of working-class and lower-class votes on the PCI and of the votes of the small and medium bourgeoisie on the DC, which creates the *bases* for a radicalization of Italian political life, especially since, with such a composition, the DC electorate seems prepared to do all to defend its material interests.[64]

With these changes, the support of traditional groups becomes more vital for the DC and the Gaullists. The axis of alliance holding together traditional and modern sectors of the economy – which was always one of the critical underpinnings of the parties of government – has now become crucial for survival. Even in the days when the DC and the Gaullists were most successful in gaining support from all classes in society, the alliance between traditional and modern sectors was a major determinant of party programs and government policy.[65] Though often obscured – especially at moments of maximum zeal for social reform – by rhetoric about productivity, innovation, and industrialization, the commitment to preserving the traditional sector did not at any time disappear altogether. The modernizing projects of the elites were never unambiguous in their prescriptions for the traditional sector. Neither the alliance between traditional and modern sectors nor the ideological frame in which the policies that nourish this alliance are set are new in France and Italy: They have been important throughout the postwar period in providing electoral stability and a certain legitimation of national government that made the mutual renunciations of the claims of traditional and modern groups acceptable.

But as the catchall parties of the sixties net smaller shares of the salaried population in the seventies, their structures, programs, and personnel come increasingly to reflect the social alliance of traditional and modern interests on which the parties now depend more heavily. In France, for example, if we consider the successive approaches to the traditional electorate of three Gaullist leaders, Charles de Gaulle, Georges Pompidou, and Jacques Chirac, the rising level of promises, concessions, and courtship is striking. Where de Gaulle pushed through reforms to modernize agriculture and commerce at the expense of traditional firms, Pompidou agreed to legislation that allows traditional commerce to control supermarket expansion and commercial development. Chirac as prime minister and now as leader of the Rassemblement pour la république (RPR) offers credits, subsidies, and even rescue from bankruptcy for small and medium-sized business, support for traditional structures in agriculture, and encouragement to a new peak organization of the middle classes (*Groupes Initiative et Responsabilité*, founded in early 1977).[66] As the traditional electorate declines, its support is more avidly sought.

In Italy, the impact of shifts in the bases of support of the DC cannot be similarly traced through shifts in policy, for the DC had never pushed its commitment to economic modernization, which in any event was a rather weak one, to the point of seriously jeopardizing traditional enterprises. Perhaps the changes in the party in the seventies are reflected in government's willingness to bail out traditional firms – with, for example, the Helfer law limiting supermarket expansion or the creation of GEPI to salvage medium-sized firms in trouble.[67] But here again, the lines of continuity with the past are too clear, and the support of the other parties for these measures too strong, to make it plausible to attribute these policies to changes in the DC social coalition.

The second major change of the past decade that has increased the power of the traditional electorate is the prospect of Left governments in countries long ruled by Center-Right coalitions. In Italy, the DC has only a 6 percent margin of votes over the PCI, and given the attrition of its old partners in the Center-Right, the DC has had in the mid-seventies to concede to the Communists a kind of right of prior consent over policy in order to remain in power. In France, in the period 1973–7 for the first time since 1958, a Left government came to seem possible, even probable. Polls at the end of 1976 showed the Socialist-Communist-Left Radical *programme commun* coalition with a substantial lead over the current majority. Even after that alliance broke apart in fall 1977 and the Left lost the March 1978 legislative elections, the chances of Left victory in the near future remained.

The narrowing margins of electoral victory have increased the weight of traditional groups in parties of both government and opposition. In part, the reasons are those just discussed: For parties in government, the fact that the numbers in the traditional sector, though relatively less important than two decades ago, are more valuable than in the past because of the defections of electors from other social strata and because of the closeness of the race. But closer Left-Right competition works to the advantage of the traditional sector in other ways as well. First, in order to recuperate voters from the ranks of the opposition, to win over independents and keep in its own camp those who are wavering, the parties of government are forced back on the tried and true themes of old battles. It is hardly surprising that the hard-pressed DC tries to revive anticommunism; or that the French Gaullists raise not only the collectivist and communist commitments of the opposition but also that hoary spector of the past, anti-clericalism. Those who, like Giscard d'Estaing or Left factions of the DC have argued for appealing to the voters with programs of social and political reform, seem already to have lost the battle over the orientation of the defense of the majority. The Gaullists in France and the DC in Italy have placed the old issues in the front lines of their electoral strategies.

Among the consequences of the revival of the old themes of conservative defense is the increased salience of the traditional sector. The old issues are so interwoven with the protection of small independent property that any resurrection of the former requires new commitments to the latter. However much the industrialists who support the Gaullists or the DC wish to replace peasant farming with modern agriculture or to sweep away small shops and put supermarkets in their place, they cannot fight a political battle against collectivism and communism without offering homage in word and deed to private property and individual enterprise. To mobilize the electorate against the *programme commun*, it is not enough to point out that banks and some dozen large corporations will be nationalized. Rather, the entire structure of small, independent ownership must be shown to be in jeopardy. And the reevocation of these issues and values inevitably mutes the call to modernization and industrialization, a political commitment in which the values associated with small private property and the protection of *les droits acquis* are far less central.

The traditional sector's political clout is enhanced by closer Left-Right contests in yet another way. One of the government's principal assets in both countries is the general fear – shared as well by many of the Left's electors and potential electors – that if the Left came to power, the reactions of its opponents and the disruption of society and economy that they would wreak would produce chaos. Put another way, the parties of the Center-Right are able to govern not only because they command electoral majorities but also because they command the balance of economic and social forces in the country. Among the factors that consolidates their hold on the electorate is the belief that the social and economic forces aligned against the Left would make its government impossible, even if it won an arithmetic electoral majority. To give credence to the claim that only the parties in the current majority can preserve enough social consensus to make the system work, it must remain plausible that the social groups represented by the parties of the Center-Right find a Left government so unacceptable an outcome that they will try to prevent it at all costs. And failing in this, they will try to undermine it after the fact. Central in this scenario, and therefore to dissuading potential defectors to the Left, is the attitude of the small, independent propertied class toward a possible Left government, for on their eventual behavior hangs much of the plausibility of the scenario of social and economic disorder.

The extreme sensitivity the government shows to the political sentiments of the traditional sector thus reflects not so much concern about losing their votes – which is quite unlikely – as concern about a slackening in their unconditional opposition to the Left in power. In France, for example, the electors of the traditional sector were among the most faithful of the Right's supporters over the period 1974–6, during which the majority suffered a serious decline in its electorate. Despite this loyalty, and the absence on the horizon of any plausible political alternative for most of the traditional middle-class electorate, the government reacted with alarm and concessions when signs of discontent and unrest appeared in the traditional sector. The organizations of the traditional sector did not – and could not convincingly – threaten to shift their electors. Rather, they warned of the decline in their supporters' violent objections to a government of the Left: They brandished the menace of their supporters' indifference. As Léon Gingembre, the long-time president of the conservative CGPME explained: When Giscard d'Estaing adopts the policies of the Left in order to win back part of the electorate, he calculates that his own voters will never desert him. But the more disaffected his electors, the more resigned they become to a government of the Left. "Instead of fighting socialism, they retreat; and there are two tendencies: *fuir en avant ou se plier trop vite.*"[68]

Though the parties of the majority did not have to worry much about losing the traditional electors, they did by the spring of 1976 confront evidence that these electors were gradually accepting the notion of life with a Left-wing government, preparing in short to *fuir en avant ou se plier trop vite.* A 1976 survey of French industrialists showed that though they were far more negative about the Socialists and Communists than the population at large, they also were more convinced of the likelihood of the Left's victory than was the general population.[69] Small and large industrialists were about equally negative in their opinions of the opposition parties, but the expectations of the industrialists about what the consequences of the Left's victory would be on their own firms and on the economy varied greatly according to firm size, with the industrialists of firms employing over

500 having consistently more pessimistic views. Since large firms have more highly unionized and politicized work forces, since they are the ones singled out for measures of nationalization and public control, this difference in perceptions on the part of large and small industrialists was understandable. What is striking, however, is the magnitude of the differences and the relative complacency of the small industrialists about the consequences for them of an event which they were far from favoring. For example, to the question of whether unions would moderate their demands if the Left won or, conversely, would become more militant, 64 percent of the industrialists from firms employing under 50 thought unions would be more moderate; only 34 percent thought that unions would be more radical. For industrialists from firms over 500, the responses were virtually reversed in proportion: 31 percent believed more union moderation likely in the event of Left victory and 65 percent feared more militancy.[70] Similarly, the larger the firm, the more likely its owner was to think that the country's problems would lead to conflict and violence, rather than be resolved by negotiation and compromise.[71]

For Italy we have no comparable survey, but there, evidence from the regions administered by the Communists, from statements by industrialists, and from their participation with Communists in various discussions on the economy all suggest the same conclusion: that while the social groups at the core of the government's majority are no more favorable than before to the Left, they are beginning to conceive of the economy and society as continuing much as always under a government of the Left and to accomodate themselves to this prospect. While the electors remain faithful, their views are changing in ways that erode the Right's hegemony, understood here in Gramsci's sense of a party's capacity to create a general societal belief that only its values, the modes of governance it practices, and the prospects it offers provide a stable foundation for government. To stop this erosion, then, which endangers their legitimacy as well as their electorate, the parties of the majority in both countries must work to retain the loyalty and commitment of even that part of its electorate which "has nowhere else to go" politically.

The parties of the Left, conversely, even when they have little chance of winning votes from the traditional electorate, must still win a certain kind of acceptance. The Left needs this in order to convince potential supporters that if elected to power, it could govern: that is, that even those social forces who oppose the Left would accept the election returns and, with whatever reluctance, adjust to the new situation. For all the historical reasons discussed here, the Italian Communist Party has been far more sensitive than the French Left to this problem of achieving legitimacy in the eyes of its opponents. The PCI's intense wooing of the traditional middle classes – stepped up as the party approaches government – can best be understood as an effort to neutralize the hostility of these groups even if not to win their votes.

The third change in the party configuration of France and Italy that has contributed to the preservation of the traditional sector's power has been increased levels of competition within the majority coalition. In the 1976 legislative elections in Italy, the DC remained the largest party only by cutting into the electorates of its frequent allies, the Liberals and the Social Democrats. In France, the 1974 election of Giscard d'Estaing (an Independent Republican) as president, with the National Assembly still in the hands of a Gaullist majority, opened up a period of heightened tension within the majority. This has been exacerbated by conflicts between Giscard d'Estaing and his one-time prime minister, the Gaullist leader Jacques Chirac, over leadership of the majority.

While the traditional electorate is unlikely to move from Right to Left, it is relatively mobile between the parties of the Right and Center. And the possibility of losing electors to another party on the *same* side of the Left-Right divide has been a serious consideration at times for both the DC and the Gaullists. For the DC, the problem was most worrisome at the height of MSI (neofascist) successes and now again acquires acuity as the DC struggles to remain the largest party. For the Gaullists, in the early years of the Fifth Republic, capturing the Right electorate from other Centrist and Right parties was a preoccupying task, and this conquest has never been a secure one: Defections of the traditional electorate to other Right and Center parties defeated the 1969 referendum on the regions and, before that, in the 1965 presidential elections, reduced de Gaulle's tally. While not a new one then, the problem of keeping the traditional electorate out of the hands of a candidate's coalition partners has acquired new relevance in the past few years in France and Italy. Like the shift in the groups that support the majority and the growing strength of the Left, the competition within the Right works to maintain an influence for the traditional electorate that its numbers alone cannot explain.

Finally, in Italy though not in France, a fourth change is at work to make the traditional sector disproportionately important for the major parties. This is the growing antisystem protest directed against the Christian Democrats and the Communists, both perceived by a significant fraction of the electorate as responsible for Italy's political and economic troubles. The successes of the Radical Party and of candidates to the Left of the PCI in the 1979 legislative elections are one indication of this disaffection with the major parties of government and opposition and terrorism may be regarded as another. Perhaps most revealing of the extent of popular discontent was the near success of the 1978 referendum in which Italians voted on whether to revoke the law on public financing of political parties. The votes for repeal (44 percent) were generally regarded as votes of no confidence in the major parties.

The parties did best in rallying their electorate to support continuing public finance in those regions of Italy where small and medium enterprises predominate – the "third Italy" of the Northeast, the Po Valley, the Center, and the Adriatic coast.[72] These regions are distinctive not only because of their traditional economies, but also because of their stable political allegiances – in some areas for the DC, in others, for the PCI. Aris Accornero argues suggestively that in both the "red" and the "white" provinces of the "third Italy" the degree of integration between the political system and the socioeconomic system worked to reduce the tensions and conflicts that in the "first Italy" (the industrial triangle) and the second (the Mezzogiorno) exploded in protest against the parties and a vote for repeal.[73] Social cohesion and the capacity to absorb and buffer the shocks of economic and political crisis are greater in these regions where the traditional economy predominates. For this reason, both major parties find here the most stable and loyal components of their electorates. Thus the political consequences of the uneven spread of antisystem protest through Italy may well be to encourage the political parties to support the traditional sector.

The shifts in French and Italian party politics discussed are currently the subject of considerable debate with substantial disagreement on the magnitude of the changes, on their origins, and on their likely outcomes. Here we intend only to suggest some of the consequences of these realignments of the party system for the political power of the traditional sector and not to consider the merits of various contending interpretations of the transformations of European politics. In juxtaposing the French and Italian cases, we do not propose that these changes in the parties are producing similar political outcomes in the two countries, nor that they have the same causes. Rather, the differences between France and Italy in the patterns of alliance within government and opposition camps, in the relative weight of parties within each camp, in party histories and strategies, and in the social bases of support of the parties seem more likely to propel French and Italian politics along divergent trajectories. What is striking, however, is that in the two countries, for all their differences, the changes of the past decade as a common result have perpetuated the political influence of the traditional sector.

Conclusions

In ways that theories of modern industrial societies did not predict, the economic and political conjunctures of the past decades have contributed to the preservation of the traditional sector. The malfunctioning of contemporary industrial societies has created new prospects for the survival and vitality of traditional "remnants." The inflexibilities of modern capitalist economies have made the maintenance and expansion of economic activity in traditional firms important. The erosion of the old bases of party support and the crumbling of the legitimizing tenets of belief that underpinned the governments of the postwar period have increased the influence of the traditional electorate. But the question of whether the traditional sector's survival is temporary or long term remains unanswered. If the uses of the traditional sector are linked to contingent economic and political difficulties, then we may continue to expect that these accidents of the short term will do no more than delay the inevitable outcome of the secular trends to modernization and industrialization, namely, elimination of the traditional sector. If, however, the uses of the traditional sector, though conjuncturally conditioned and elicited, are linked to permanent structural properties of modern industrial societies, then the fate of the traditional sector remains open.

The variety of evidence we have presented of the traditional sector's role not only in times of prosperity but in recession, of the sector's importance not only for those it supports in politics but for those it opposes, and of its functions as a buffer or shock absorber in the recurrent tensions and conflicts of modern society – all suggest more than the notion of a delayed demise for the sector can readily be stretched to accommodate. More significantly, the range of problems in contemporary European societies for which the traditional sector offers some compensatory remedy cannot be adequately explained as conjunctural. Even leaving in abeyance here the issue of whether the recurrent economic crises of contemporary capitalist economies are implicit in the system itself, other problems for which the traditional structures offer solutions are clearly part and parcel of modern societies. If we consider unionization or increased capital investment or the demise of political ideologies and parties linked to the secularization crisis of the nineteenth century or to the battle over communism in the twentieth, these economic, social, and political processes are rooted in the logic of modernization and industrialization and can hardly be treated as accidents.

Put another way, to understand whether the survival of the traditional sector is temporary or long term requires going back and reexamining fundamental assumptions about industrial societies. The dominant models of these societies depend, on the one hand, on the assumption of an integration and homogenization of society with the progressive extension of modern industrial technologies and, on the other, on the assumption that solutions for the problems and conflicts of contemporary societies lie in the further development of the same processes that generated these societies. On these two premises hangs the prediction of the disappearance of the traditional sector. It is, however, not only the traditional sector that appears as a peripheral phenomenon in industrial societies on these assumptions; the significance of a wide range of institutions like stratification by race and by sex or foreign workers in the economy in this perspective is also shown to be more transitional and circumstantial than long term. These two assumptions make it impossible to recognize the critical role in contemporary societies – not only and not everywhere of the traditional sector – but of diverse phenomena having in common only the anomaly of their presence and salience for industrial society: anomalous because their origins lie outside the characteristic structures and processes of industrialization and modernization. To begin to construct a view of the world that places these phenomena in the core of the explanation and not at its periphery, the final chapter reconsiders the assumptions that underlie our theories of industrial societies.

NOTES

1. On the Japanese case, see Ronald Dore, *British Factory, Japanese Factory* (Berkeley: University of California Press, 1973).
2. On the correlations between firm size and the other factors in the traditional/backwardness complex, see, for example, the study of Italian firms, Mediocredito Centrale, *Lineamenti dell' industria manifatturiera italiana* (Rome: 1972), pp. 34–9. Dore, in *British Factory, Japanese Factory* also points to firm size as critical. The measures of firm size – output, number employed, and so forth – are all highly intercorrelated, and various studies have concluded that it does not make much difference which one is used. This matter is discussed in Dean Savage, *Founders, Heirs and Managers: French Industrial Leadership in Transition* (Beverly Hills, California: Sage, 1979).
3. In France, artisanal firms were legally defined (decree of 1 March 1962) by size as those in which the firm employs fewer than five workers, excluding family members and apprentices, and by nature of activity. Various legislative texts delimit the category "small and medium business" in

France: a 11 June 1968 decree that opened special borrowing facilities for firms with a volume of trade under 20 million francs; a 17 August 1967 decree that set up a scheme for employee profit sharing in firms with over 100 employees; a 27 December 1968 law requiring that all firms employing over 50 workers allow the organization of a union section, and others. See Bernard Brizay, *Le Patronat: histoire, structure, stratégie du CNPF* (Paris: Editions du Seuil, 1975), pp. 290–3. The criteria established in each case are somewhat different but have wide areas of overlap. The single national trade association representing small and medium business (Confédération Générale des Petites et Moyennes Entreprises et du Patronat Réel) defines these firms as "those in which the head of the firm is personally and directly responsible for the financial, technical, social, and moral commitments of the firm, no matter what its juridical status." Though size does not figure here, nonetheless, the requirement for the industrialist's personal commitment is such as to make this definition coincide roughly with those of the legislative texts (from Confédération Générale des Petites et Moyennes Entreprises et du Patronat Réel, Documentation, "Définition permanente des P.M.E.," January 1976).

4. On this point, see Arno J. Mayer, "The Lower Middle Class as Historical Problem," *Journal of Modern History, 47* (September 1975), no. 3.
5. On the replacement of traditional firms by new ones that are essentially the same, see Frank Bechhofer and Brian Elliott, "Persistence and Change: the Petite Bourgeoisie in Industrial Society," *Archives européennes de sociologie, 17* (1976), no. 1.
6. See, for example, Claude Servolin, "L'Absorption de l'agriculture dans le mode de production capitaliste," in Y. Tavernier, M. Gervais, and C. Servolin, *L'Univers politique des paysans dans la France contemporaine* (Cahiers de la Fondation Nationale des Sciences Politiques, no. 184. Paris: Colin, 1972).
7. For an attempt to reconstruct the small independent propertied class out of census data, see Paolo Sylos-Labini, *Saggio sulle classi sociali* (Bari: Laterza, 1975), pp. 153–60.
8. Claude Quin, *Classes sociales et union du peuple de France* (Paris: Editions sociales, 1976), p. 35. *Recensement général agricole, 1955, 1970,* cited in F. Clavaud et al., *Quelle agriculture pour la France?* (Paris: Editions sociales, 1974), annexes.
9. Corrado Barberis, "Men, Farms and Product in Italian Agriculture," in Banco di Roma, *Review of the Economic Conditions in Italy* (September 1971) Vol. XXV, no. 5, p. 402.
10. Atti parlamentari, Legislatura V, Senato della Repubblica, Ministro del Bilancio e della Programmazione Economica, *Relazione generale sulla situazione economica del Paese,* 1970 (Rome: 1971), Vol. I, p. 6.
11. Speech by Yvon Bourges, Minister of Commerce and Artisanry, reported in *Le Monde* (15 February 1973).

12. Carlo Fabrizi, "La razionalizzazione del commercio italiano in rapporto all'urbanistico commerciale," *Atti del congresso internazionale commercio e urbanistica* (14–16 October 1967), p. 62.
13. Quin (1976), 118–19.
14. "L'Artisanat et le secteur des métiers," from *Revue économique de la Banque nationale de Paris* (April 1973), reprinted in *Problèmes économiques* (13 June 1973), p. 4.
15. Michael Didier and Edouard Malinvaud, "La concentration de l'industrie s'est-elle accentuée depuis le début du siècle?" *Economie et statistique* (June 1969), no. 2, p. 7.
16. Savage (1979), 69.
17. *Le Nouvel Economiste* (24 November 1975).
18. Giorgio Ruffolo, *Il ruolo delle piccole e medie industrie nella strategia programmatica,* Rome (27 October 1971), p. 3.
19. Didier and Malinvaud (1969), p. 6.
20. Annie Kriegel, "L'Evolution de l'artisanat dans le 3eme arrt de Paris de 1896 à 1945" (unpublished D.E.S. memoir, Paris, 1947). Part IV, Ch. 2.
21. FLM, Sindacato provinciale di Bologna, *Ristrutturazione e organizzazione del lavoro* (Rome: Edizioni SEUSI, nd), see especially Ch. 2, pp. 44, 53.
22. Studies cited in Giorgio Fuà, *Occupazione e capacità produttiva: la realtà italiana* (Bologna: Il Mulino, 1976), pp. 32–3.
23. *La Repubblica* (8 February 1978).
24. Recent work by Massimo Paci develops this point brilliantly, arguing that one must explain both the "demand" for the functions the traditional sector performs and the "supply," that is, the availability in some countries and not in others of institutions like the small family firm that can be used for these purposes. The essays in this volume, like most of the literature on this theme, focus on the first of these problems. Paci's new research on the history of the family in certain regions of Italy, where the family has played a critical role in regulating the passage of its members from agrarian to industrial activities, suggests how the second task ought to be approached. Massimo Paci, "Alcune riflessioni sui fattori sociali dello sviluppo della piccola impresa industriale e artigiana nelle Marche," seminar paper presented 18 November 1978; and "Struttura e funzioni della famiglia nello sviluppo capitalistico 'periferico'," 1978 (publication forthcoming).
25. Kriegel (1947).
26. See Bernard Guibert et al., *La Mutation industrielle de la France* (Paris: Institut National de la Statistique et des Etudes Economiques, 1975), Vol. 2, pp. 40–1.
27. There are national surveys of wage disparities across the country for similar work performed in firms of different sizes in different regions, but these surveys are not publically available.

128   *A political approach*

28. For example, Serge Dassault (of the Dassault aircraft company) explained before the Social and Economic Council: "Subcontracting allows us to produce at lower cost. . . . Actually, we profit from the more flexible and simpler organization of our subcontractors who have much lower hourly wages: In France we find firms whose hourly wages are half ours!" For a discussion of the role of wage differentials in subcontracting in France, see A. Sallez and J. Schlegel, *La Sous-traitance dans l'industrie* (Paris: Dunod, 1963).

29. See a review of this research by Judith Chubb, "The Functions of Economic 'Marginality': The Case of Italian Industry," Unpublished M.I.T. Department of Political Science paper, September 1975. On these questions in the fifties, see the report of the parliamentary inquiry commission, the "Rubinacci commission," in *Relazioni della commissione parlamentare di inchiesta sulle condizioni dei lavoratori in Italia (1964)*, Vol. 7. Two excellent studies have appeared after the Chubb literature review: one of the metalworking industries in Bergamo province, Federazione lavoratori metalmeccanici [FLM] *Sindacato e piccola impresa* (Bari: De Donato, 1975); one on metalworking industries in Bologna province, FLM, *Ristrutturazione e organizzazione del lavoro* (Rome: Edizioni Società Editrice Unitaria Sindacale, nd), Vol. 1.

30. From a 1974 study, Centro studi Federlibro-FLM-SISM, Confederazione italiana sindacati lavoratori di Verona, *Piccola azienda grande sfruttamento*, cited in FLM, *Sindacato e piccola impresa*, p. 96.

31. Comune di Modena, "Il lavoro a domicilio nel quartiere Madonnina" (1971), p. 79.

32. These studies are cited in Giorgio Fuà (1976), pp. 32–3.

33. Vera Lutz, *Italy: A Study in Economic Development* (London, Oxford University Press, 1962); George Hildebrand, *Growth and Structure in the Economy of Modern Italy* (Cambridge: Harvard University Press, 1965), particularly in Ch. 14; and Giorgio Fuà (1976).

34. Savage (1979).

35. On the shifts of women in and out of the labor force in response to increased demand see, Fiorella Padoa Schioppa, *La forza lavora femminile* (Bologna: Il Mulino, 1977) pp. 20–6.

36. On the change in the composition of the Northern Italian work force and the expulsion of "nonprime" workers from good jobs, see Massimo Paci, *Mercato del lavoro e classi sociali in Italia* (Bologna: Il Mulino, 1973).

37. For France, see Sallez and Schlegel (1963) and Jean-Jacques Stefanelly, "Les Problèmes posés par la sous-traitance," report presented to the Conseil économique et social (21 March 1973), reprinted in *Problèmes économiques* (13 June 1973). For Italy, see references in note 29.

38. Marcello Marin, "La distribuzione in Italia," *Nord e Sud*, (1971), no. 2, 70. S. Ravalli, "La distribuzione al dettaglio," *Mondo economico* (23 December 1967).

39. Ugo Maggioli, *Contributo per l'analisi e la previsione dell'evoluzione delle forze di lavoro agricole in Lombardia* (Milan: Giunta Regionale Lombarda, 1971), p. 1.
40. Sylos-Labini (1975), pp. 153–60.
41. Alessandro Pizzorno, "I ceti medi nei meccanismi del consenso," in F. Cavazza and S. Graubard, *Il caso italiano* (Milan: Garzanti, 1974), p. 326. Trans. of passage by S. Berger.
42. On the small firm as a channel for social mobility in France see Nonna Mayer, "Une filière de mobilité ouvrière: l'accès à la petite entreprise artisanale et commerciale," *Revue française de sociologie* 18 (1977); Nonna Mayer, "Les Petits commerçants français: un declin limité (1906– 75)," Paper presented at Conference of Europeanists, March 29–31, 1978, Washington, D.C.; and Daniel Bertaux and Isabelle Bertaux-Wiame, "Artisanal Bakery in France. How it lives and why it survives," in Frank Bechhofer and Brian Elliott, *The Petty Bourgeoisie* (London: Macmillan, 1980).
43. Sylos-Labini (1975), pp. 153–60 and Tables 7.3, 7.4.
44. For the Italian Communist Party's analysis of and program for small business, see the papers and debates of a 1974 party conference in Istituto Gramsci-CESPE, *La piccola e la media industria nella crisi dell'economia italiana* (Rome: Editori Riuniti, 1975), Vols. 1 and 2. See also Stephen Hellman, "The PCI's Alliance Strategy and the Case of the Middle Classes," in D. L. M. Blackmer and S. Tarrow (eds.), *Communism in Italy and France* (Princeton: Princeton University Press, 1975).
45. *L'Unità* (18 September 1971).
46. Pierre Poujade's movement was the Union de Défense des Commerçants et Artisans (UDCA); Nicoud's, a merger of the Comité d'Information et de Défense (CID) with the Union Nationale de Travailleurs Indépendants (UNATI); Léon Gingembre, president of the Confédération générale des Petites et Moyennes Entreprises (CGPME) launched in 1975 a Union des Chefs et Responsables d'Entreprise (UNICER).
47. This argument is developed in Suzanne Berger, "D'une boutique à l'autre: Changes in the Organization of the Traditional Middle Classes from Fourth to Fifth Republics," *Comparative Politics* (October 1977).
48. Stanley Hoffmann, *Le Mouvement Poujade* (Cahiers de la Fondation Nationale des Sciences Politiques, no. 81. Paris: Colin, 1956), p. 22.
49. On the Poujade movement, the best account remains Hoffmann (1956).
50. On the CID-UNATI, see Gérard Nicoud, *Les Dernières libertés . . . menottes aux mains* (Paris: Denoël, 1972); André Bonnet, "Un nouveau groupe de pression: Le CID-UNATI," *Revue politique et parlementaire* (June–July 1973), nos. 843–5; Georges Lefranc, *Les Organisations patronales en France* (Paris: Payot, 1976); and Berger (1977).
51. Nicoud (1972), pp. 82–3. Trans. of passage by S. Berger.
52. *Loi d'orientation pour le commerce et l'artisanat,* known as the "Royer

law," for Jean Royer, the Minister of Commerce and Artisanry, responsible not only for its passage, but for conceiving some of its most controversial corporatist features.

53. More authorizations were denied (238) than granted (222) in that year. *Le Monde* (3 January 1975).

54. From a survey by the Ministry of Economy and Finance, reported in *Le Monde* (21 January 1977).

55. See, for example, the thin treatment of small and medium firms in the *Programme commun;* the virtual absence of discussion of such enterprises in a major debate over the Socialist platform for industry, reprinted in *Les Socialistes face aux patrons* (Paris: L'Expansion/Flammarion, 1977). The most recent authoritative Communist treatment of these classes is Claude Quin, *Classes sociales et union du peuple de France* (Paris: Editions Sociales, 1976) whose analysis (pp. 104–28) still focuses on the question of whether these groups are producers and exploited or exploiters. For analysis of these groups from a far-left perspective, see Christian Baudelot, Roger Establet, Jacques Malemort, *La Petite bourgeoisie en France* (Paris: Maspero, 1974) and Nicos Poulantzas, *Les Classes sociales dans le capitalisme aujourd'hui* (Paris: Seuil, 1974).

56. Otto Kirchheimer, "The Transformation of the Western European Party System," in J. La Palombara and M. Weiner, *Political Parties and Political Development* (Princeton: Princeton University Press, 1966), pp. 184–92.

57. On this, see Jean Charlot, *Le Phénomène Gaulliste* (Paris: Fayard, 1970) pp. 67–72.

58. Sylos-Labini (1974), Table 7.4. See also Mattei Dogan's estimates for 1958 in his "Political Cleavage and Social Stratification in France and Italy," in S. M. Lipset and S. Rokkan, *Party Systems and Voter Alignments* (New York: Free Press, 1967).

59. Kirchheimer (1966), p. 187.

60. The figures on the composition of the Gaullist electorate in 1965 are for the UNR party alone; for 1973 and 1976 for the majority: the Gaullists plus the Independent Republicans and Centrists. The 1965 and 1973 statistics are from IFOP and SOFRES surveys cited in Suzanne Berger, *The French Political System* (New York: Random House, 1974); 1976 statistics from a SOFRES survey after the 1976 cantonal elections, "Les français et les élections cantonales."

61. On the widening gap between religious belief and political practice, it is significant that while 67 percent of respondents in a 1953 survey judged that one could not be a "good Communist and a good Catholic at the same time," by 1970 this figure had dropped to 44 percent and by 1972 to 34 percent. Cited in Giacomo Sani, "Secular Trends and Party Realignments in Italy: The 1975 Elections," Paper presented at the APSA convention (September 1975), p. 25.

62. See Arturo Parisi and Gianfranco Pasquino, "Relazioni e partiti-elettorie tipi di voto," in A. Parisi and G. Pasquino, *Continuità e mutamento elettorale in Italia* (Bologna: Il Mulino, 1977).

63. Giacomo Sani, "The Italian Election in 1976: Continuity and Change," Paper prepared for Conference Group on Italian Politics, APSA (September 1976). Also, G. Sani, "Generations and Politics in Italy," Paper presented at Fondazione Luigi Einaudi, Turin (March 1977).

64. Arturo Parisi and Gianfranco Pasquino, "20 giugno: struttura politica e comportamento elettorale," in Parisi and Pasquino (1977); trans. of passage by S. Berger. Until more current surveys of the Italian electorate become available, it remains difficult to know to what extent the DC's interclassist base has been reduced, but the studies reported by Parisi and Pasquino and a variety of single constituency studies suggest significant changes.

65. For a brilliant analysis of the relations between traditional and modern groups in Italian parties, see Michele Salvati, "L'Origine della crisi in corso," *Quaderni Piacentini*, 11 (March 1972), 46.

66. Though bailing out big businesses in trouble was no novelty in the Fifth Republic, rescuing small and medium-sized firms was. During Chirac's tenure of office, several new mechanisms were created to help them: Departmental-level commissions and an interministerial committee (*Comité interministeriel pour l'aménagement des structures industrielles*).

67. Gestioni e partecipazione industriale (GEPI).

68. Interview with Léon Gingembre, April 15, 1976. The quote may be roughly translated as "to escape forward or to give in too quickly."

69. SOFRES survey, 10–24 September 1976, of 500 industrialists, reprinted in *Les Socialistes face aux patrons* (1977), p. 207.

70. *Ibid.*, pp. 211, 215.

71. *Ibid.*, p. 215.

72. Arnaldo Bagnasco, *Tre Italie. La problematica territoriale dello sviluppo italiano.* (Bologna: Il Mulino, 1977).

73. Aris Accornero, "Nella 'terza Italia' maggiore coesione," *Rinascita* (23 June 1978).

5

DISCONTINUITY IN THE POLITICS OF INDUSTRIAL SOCIETY

A century and a half after the Industrial Revolution, the coexistence of traditional and modern groups continues in most of Western Europe. In a few countries, the traditional sector has been reduced to vestigial proportions, but in others there remain numerically significant and politically influential groups whose technologies, modes of management, and values are traditional. This survival is a fact that has been explained away more than explained. Implicit in the theories that have shaped our understanding of industrial societies is the inevitable decline and disappearance of the traditional sector and the notion that the traditional firms that remain are only remnants. And yet, as the preceding chapter has argued, neither the operation of the economy nor the pattern of politics in many of the societies called advanced industrial or postindustrial can be understood without the traditional sector.

What we must account for is the critical role in the functioning and evolution of contemporary societies of a variety of institutions whose origins and modes of operation fall *outside* the range of explanation of the theories we have used to identify the salient structures of modern societies. The organization of politics, economy, and society around the conflicts and alliances created by the survival of traditional groups, or by ethnicity, or by race are all anomalous phenomena in the dominant models of industrial society. To understand why this is so, why these issues are barely intelligible in the conventional paradigm of industrial society, is the first purpose of this chapter. The second is to suggest the new assumptions on which a theory might be built that would bring these phenomena into sharp focus.

132

Theories of industrial society

Society and economy

The two main routes to understanding contemporary societies have been traced by liberal and Marxist theories, and despite all differences, both share a common conception of the unity of mature industrial societies. By liberals here we mean a diverse group of theorists that includes social philosophers like Saint-Simon and Herbert Spencer as well as most contemporary social scientists writing on economic and political development. What they have in common is the belief that the fundamental character of industrial society is determined by particular technologies and by the social relationships and groups that they generate. This view they share with the Marxists, however much they may differ on other critical points. For Marxists and liberals, to simplify greatly, an industrial society comes into being as technologies based on machine production in large-scale factories for mass markets spread through the economy and generate a capitalist and a working class. At the beginning of the industrial era, factory-based modes of production coexisted with older modes of production; capitalists and proletarians lived in a society with artisans and peasants, but this mixed society of the industrial economy gradually gave way to a unified and mature industrial society.

In these theories, the unitary character of industrial society is created in two ways. First, industrialization generates processes that integrate society by extending the economic mechanisms and social relationships that prevail at the center out into the peripheries, thus pulling all of society into the relationships that characterize its most advanced sectors. The most important of these integrative mechanisms in both liberal and Marxist theory is the market, for it is through competition that more backward enterprises and the groups working in them are defeated and absorbed or else transformed to resemble firms of the typical industrial model. Liberal theories underline the importance, alongside the market, of other processes of integration inherent in industrialization that promote the gradual homogenization of society. Increasing mobility among social groups – from country to city, from periphery to center – wipes out the traces of regional particularisms and of isolating group cultures. Improved communication, as highways, railroads, telephone, and mass media break down the social distances among groups, also works to create a society in which the dominant axis of economic and social organization is based on the industrial economy and on the values, hierarchies, and social constraints that it generates.

In liberal theories about industrial society, these processes of integration are seen as leading to a gradual reduction of the conflict in society. As society is simplified to the relationships which derive from the industrial economy, authority and power which once were exercised on the basis of tradition, conquest, and compulsion are legitimated by competence, expertise, and productivity; the natural relationships among the social classes of an industrial society are cooperative and complementary. On the contrary, for Marxists, the crystallization of society into the groupings based on the relations of production in the industrial economy will produce a polarization of society leading to more and more antagonistic relations among groups and higher levels of conflict. The natural relationship among industrial classes is class conflict. But for the Marxists as much as for the liberals, the relationship among the dominant classes of the industrial order implies a critical similarity between the two sides. However irreconcilable the conflicts of interest between capitalists and proletarians, Marxists see these as the kind of conflicts that arise between two parties with different stakes within the same socioeconomic system. However intense the clash of values, they are the kind of clashes that result from the exercise of the same forms of rationality by groups occupying different positions in the same system. Capitalists and workers have something in common – even in their battles – that neither of them shares with artisans or shopkeepers or peasants. The objectives and strategies of action of the former are essentially determined by the industrial structures in which they operate, while the latter groups remain attached to different systems of economic organization and different orders of economic and social rationality.

In sum, the unitary character of industrial society, which is the overarching structure in liberal and Marxist thought, derives from the processes of integration immanent in industrialization that tend to iron out the differences that societies inherit from their pasts and from the fundamental similarities of the principal social groups in an industrial economy. In the case of liberal theories, these similarities lead to cooperation, whereas in the case of Marxism, they are predicted to produce conflict; but for our present purposes, these differences are less important than the fact that for both theories the axis of cooperation or conflict revolves about issues and stakes generated wholly within the industrial system.

Other groups – those with origins in the past like the peasants and those with origins in some noneconomic cleavage in society like ethnicity – can continue to exist or may even begin in a mature industrial society. But the dominant groups, those who are economically and socially the "most advanced" and therefore ultimately the decisive elements, are the ones generated by their relationship to the central structures of the industrial system. The quarrels between Marxists and liberals over the role of the white-collar workers, the new working class, or managers is a controversy in which both sides' common point of departure is that the significant social classes are those which arise in relation to basic changes in the economy. The points in dispute arise over the identification of the new structural mechanisms in the economy and over specification of the groups that they generate.

For both of these camps, society is going somewhere, and where is determined by groups with a definably common relationship to the emerging structures of the new society. Other groups continue to appear or survive, but between them and the dominant social groups, relationships are essentially contingent and alliances temporary. In fact, the power attributed to such groups – in the main, leftovers from the preindustrial past – is that of hindering and slowing down the wave of the future.

When political development theorists have considered the question of whether the traditional sector might survive alongside the modern one, they have typically concluded that even where economic, ethnic, or other dualisms exist, the processes of integration will result in the emergence of "a structurally more simplified and better integrated society."[1] In a typical formulation of this point, Bert Hoselitz has argued:

Changes in social structure are closely based, in my opinion, on changes in the nature and conditions of economic growth, and on the whole the basic processes of economic growth are very similar in all developing countries. What varies among these peoples are certain cultural conditions, most of which are inherited from a long past. Though in its intermediate phases the type of stratification associated with economic growth may appear to be dualistic, it is also compatible with quite different cultural conditions, and in the next few decades systems of stratification in different Asian and African countries should become increasingly similar.[2]

In treating the same issues, Gabriel Almond concludes that premodern structures may survive indefinitely within a modern society, but what he defines as premodern in this context are primary structures and attachments as opposed to secondary ones.[3] Though he recognizes that the presence of traditional structures is more than transitional, the relationship between modern and traditional elements is a static one with little significance for the shape and direction of social development.

In Marxism as well, the major theorists have predicted the expansion of the capitalist system to absorb and to transform precapitalist remnants and the emergence of a homogeneous social and economic system. As Karl Kautsky stated it, in a fashion strikingly similar to Hoselitz's cited above, "society is organic . . . and as such, must be organized in a unitary way. It is absurd to think that in a society one part could develop in one direction and another part, just as important, in the opposite direction. Society can only develop in one way."[4] This view has now come under attack in certain contemporary Marxist writings, and a new formulation of the relationship between capitalist structures of production and structures of production that remain from the feudal system (peasant, artisanal) has been advanced.[5] Far from wiping out precapitalist formations, the argument runs, capitalism exploits, preserves, and recreates them. The nature of capitalism is not to create a homogeneous world social and economic system, but rather to dominate and to draw profit from the diversity and inequality that remain in permanence. As Kostas Vergopoulos has put it, "The vital force of the capitalist system does not derive from its expanded reproduction into zones which are 'exterior' to it, but from its domination of these nonhomogeneous, irregular, nonidentical spaces."[6] But in this version, as in the Marxist theories that preceded it, the nature of the capitalist system itself is not altered by the fact of its coexistence with and exploitation of the precapitalist structures.

Politics of industrial societies

In liberal and Marxist theories, the notion of the dominance of groups associated with the central structures of the industrial economy is buttressed by a particular view of politics and the state. For those who accept the unitary conception of society sketched previously, there have been, broadly speaking, two ways of conceptualizing politics. One set of theorists (and here most of the Marxists and most of the early liberals fit in) see the state as essentially the emanation of social and economic relationships and politics as a struggle over the stakes produced by the industrial system. Within this family of ideas coexist analyses that are considerably different from each other in many other respects. Even within Marxist thought, the controversy on the role of the state is considerable, and in some versions, that of Gramsci, for example, the autonomy of politics is so great that the distinction between economic structure and political superstructure tends to disappear.[7] Still, however loosely attached the state is to the dominant classes of industrial society in these theories, the degree of autonomy is never such as to suggest that the state itself determines and shapes social groups and the economic structures of society. Rather, society is conceived of as prior to politics and as deriving its central features from social and economic factors, not from political ones. The state is necessary only in the sense that it is required to carry out certain functions that society cannot autonomously perform. The state steps in to meet social needs, settle conflicts, and otherwise respond to problems generated in society. It has, according to the theory in hand, more or less autonomy in how it does so. But in none of the theories does the state itself have a primary impact on social and economic development. The state may facilitate and speed up modernization, but it does not thereby alter in any significant way the end results of the process.

The second view of politics that accompanies these theories of social development is one held by a number of liberals. In contrast to the previous view in which the state appears as a reflection of the dominant economic relationships, in this perspective, the state and politics have considerable autonomy from society and economy, may be remarkably resistant to social and economic changes, and may even evolve in directions that are contradictory to the major trends in society. This view is most fully developed in writings on postindustrial society, where a veritable decoupling of politics and society is predicted. Samuel Huntington, in an essay on postindustrial politics, identifies the dominant lines of change in society as it moves from an industrial to postindustrial stage and predicts that politics in the future, instead of integrating the new society and responding to the needs of a postindustrial world, may be fueled by passions and values that are profoundly disintegrative.[8] Daniel Bell, in *The Coming of Post-Industrial Society*, describes the changes in economy, technology, and occupational structure that are characteristic of postindustrial society and maintains that these do not determine any particular set of changes in the state but, rather, set up the problems to which solutions need to be found.[9] But in neither of these two theorists nor in other liberal speculation on industrial and postindustrial society is there any exploration of the impact of the state on the development of society and economy. Even in those views which allow for a looseness of fit between state and economy, and at the extreme, in the conceptions of this as a virtual decoupling of the processes of economic and social development from those of political development, there is no theory of the ways in which politics determines, creates, and maintains particular social and economic patterns. However free the state may be in these theories, it is also ultimately impotent to change the course of social development. Paradoxically, the state's impact on society is better recognized in those variants of the theories that see a closer link between economic and political processes than in those that start from a premise of political autonomy.

In the views of the state associated with these liberal and Marxist theories of industrial societies, the power of traditional groups appears insignificant. When the state is conceived of as the arm of the dominant economic groups, the traditional forces figure only as an obstacle to be removed by economic progress and political domination. In the versions that accord more autonomy to political processes, the traditional groups might, in principle, have a wider range of influence in the state. But as long as politics is regarded as relatively impotent in inflecting the direction and content of social development, it is difficult to foresee a situation in which the traditional groups maintain significant power at the state level while losing out systematically in society. Or rather, such a situation can be imagined but only as one of short duration, without lasting impact on the ultimate shape of society. For example, liberal analyses of the causes of fascism and nazism have underscored the role of traditional groups. Consistent with this explanation of fascism by the "incomplete modernization" of society, these interpretations conclude by finding little long-term impact of the fascist "episode" on subsequent development. While such explanations allow for the importance of traditional groups, they assume that they are condemned to disappear soon, that their period of influence is therefore short, and that the long-term effects of their actions are bound to be outweighed by natural consequences of economic and social evolution.

Change

Finally, common to Marxist and liberal social theories is a conception of history that distinguishes sharply between, on the one side, normal, mature periods when the social and economic hegemony of a given mode of production and of the social classes associated with it is securely established and, on the other, periods of transition. All theories of history require some system of periodization; what is particular to the ones we are considering is the radical distinction between mature stages, in which the domination of given groups makes outcomes relatively predictable, and transitional stages, which are periods of relative indeterminacy. In transitional phases, the dynamic of social change is a contest between the forces of the old society that are struggling to maintain the status quo and to restore their position and the groups representative of the emerging order, which are attempting to consolidate their power. The indeterminacy of the period derives from the fact that both old and new technologies, old and new social classes, and old and new ruling groups coexist and compete, and one social order has no longer (and the new social order has not yet) the strength to overcome its adversary. It is the situation vividly described by Karl Marx in the *The Eighteenth Brumaire of Louis Bonaparte*, where French society of the mid-nineteenth century is analyzed in terms of the vectors of force exerted by groups belonging to heterogeneous economic orders, no one of which was strong enough to impose its own preferred government.

In liberal theories of economic and political development, as in *The Eighteenth Brumaire*, the indeterminacy of the transition in no way prejudices the ultimate outcome. The rise to power of Napoleon III is a bizarre resolution of a struggle for power in a transitional period, and with respect to the course of history and to the character of the mature industrial society which is emerging, Napoleon III makes no difference and his rule will not shape the mature phase that follows. This conclusion is substantially the same as that reached by the political development theorists who, after recognizing the weight of cultural and historical differences in the process of modernization, conclude with Hoselitz that in the long run the similarities inherent in the course of economic change will result in a convergence of social systems and an erasing of the differences that derive from different pasts. In transitional periods, then, the battle between the past and the future may produce outcomes in which local particularisms are triumphant, in which economic activities condemned by technological progress gain new strength, in which political elites struggling to preserve the old order appear successful. But these victories are all temporary and of no durable significance for the character of the period that eventually emerges out of this contest between old and new.

In the transitional periods, the dynamic of change is the competition between heterogeneous social forces; in contrast, in the mature periods, social change in theories we are considering is the product either of a process of working out of immanent properties of the society or of society's efforts at adaptation and reequilibration when put under strain by exogenous pressures. Marxist theory has developed the first line of explanation, Marx's account of the disintegration of capitalism being an analysis of how forces inherent in the capitalist system of production ultimately become contradictory, and the very mechanisms which made the system work become responsible for its explosion. The forces of production (technologies) change, while the relations of production (class relations, ownership) lag and conflict between the two spheres becomes acute. In its theoretical formulation, as John Plamenatz and others have pointed out, this explanation has difficulties, first because the boundaries between forces of production and relations of production shift in Marx's writings,[10] and indeed it is difficult to see how anyone could define the limits of each once and for all. Secondly, the theory – while it argues for the determining force of the mode of production, which should mean that changes in this sphere produce corresponding shifts in ownership and distribution – also attributes the principal source of conflict and system breakdown to the fact that change in the former sphere is *not* translated into changes in the second. While it would be possible to admit lags in the process of change without losing the force of the claim about the determining nature of the forces of production, it seems difficult to make the entire explanation of revolutionary breakdown depend on lag in a system that otherwise hangs together by causal determination.

In any event, these theoretical difficulties in the explanation of change have never been put to the test, since in all contemporary revolutions, the forces of change that had developed within society have received a massive assist from a major shock from outside. The wars which shattered the status quo in Russia and China may not have created the revolutions they unleashed, but by paralyzing the old society's modes of reaction and self-defense, they did destroy a certain equilibrium, or deadlock, and create the opportunity for new forces already at work within the old society to triumph. In sum, while Marxist theory leans heavily on an explanation of change through the working out of tendencies and conflict immanent in the old society, this explanation has both theoretical and practical limitations which have resulted in a doubling of the original theory with a theory of the revolutionary potential of externally generated societal crises.

This second type of explanation of change of mature societies has been the one at the heart of liberal theories and has been developed most clearly in one set of them, the systems theories. In these theories, states are analyzed as highly integrated social wholes, and the environment in which systems exist is seen as the source of the shocks and strains which compel change. As Gabriel Almond and B. Bingham Powell put it, "We need to take a major analytical step if we are to build political development more explicitly into our approach to the study of political systems. We need to look at political systems as whole entities shaping and being shaped by their environments."[11] The notion of societies as "whole entities" here, as in other variants of the liberal theories, implies that the groups within society relate to each other in ways that basically reinforce social equilibrium and stability and not in ways that engender the kind of conflicts that might transform the system. Though the external origin of the forces leading to change is most clearly spelled out by the systems theorists, it is implicit in most of the modernization literature. The processes of secularization, rationalization, and modernization are treated as essentially exogenous forces that sweep over and transform societies.

Groups, values, and institutions inherited from the past, which play a significant role in transitional periods, play virtually none in the mature phases of social development. Whether in the Marxist theory which foresees change as resulting from the contradictions immanent in each social order or in the liberal theories which regard societies as highly integrated and change as of external origin, there is no room for a dynamic in which interactions among heterogenous strata of society are significant motors of social change. Neither Marxists nor liberals would deny the existence of conflicts and alliances among traditional and modern groups in the mature stages of industrial society: only that they have significance in shaping the character of society and politics and the direction of change. The unitary conception of society that underpins Marxist and liberal explanations of how societies are organized, of the relationships between politics and society, and of change, systematically obscures the importance of what societies inherit from the past. On these grounds, there have been various critiques of the conceptualization of traditionalism, but, like Gusfield's attack on the seven fallacies about traditional society in modernization theory, they conclude that the notion can be revised without sacrificing the basic theories.[12]

We suggest, on the contrary, that it is not possible to explain the persistence and importance of the traditional sector without altering the central assumptions on which the unitary models of society build. It is not traditional survivals as such that these theories are incapable of explaining, but rather, the entire range of phenomena that derives from the heterogeneity of mature industrial societies. Cleavages between traditional and modern groups, cleavages rooted in race, region, ethnicity, and language all are described by the unitary theories of industrial society as bases of social and economic organization that have less and less weight and disappear in modern societies. From such a perspective, it is difficult to see these phenomena, let alone to evaluate their importance.

The visibility and intelligibility of these phenomena requires an angle of vision on society in which discontinuities and heterogeneity in the forms of economic and social organization and values are regarded as permanent and not transient parts of the industrial landscape. It is true that important segments of society are closely related in ways that can appropriately be conceptualized with models of economic determinism or with systems approaches. But these integrated segments do not at all times, not even in mature industrial societies, dominate social development. Alongside these integrated segments coexist on a permanent basis groups and institutions whose activities, values, and structures grow out of a matrix or matrices fundamentally different from that which produced integration in the modern and technologically advanced part of society.

This new perspective has an intellectual affinity with the theory of dualism developed by Julius Boeke in his studies of Indonesia and Michael Piore's models of labor market dualism.[13] Like both of them, it emphasizes the significance and permanence of social segmentation, the need to explore the mutually dependent relationship between the segments, and the problem of replacing a linear theory of development with an explanation of how change in each of the segments and change in the whole proceed. In our view, what is critical in these dualist theories is the notion of segmentation, and not the number of segments: two, three, or more are consistent with the structure of the argument. The number could not, however, be too large without tending to recreate the continuous array of variation of a unitary social model. Equally, social segmentation does not rule out some mobility between sectors, so long as the volume and character of this mobility still permits the maintenance within each segment of different values, rules, and institutions.

If we shift the angle of vision of analysis to place in sharp focus the discontinuous and heterogeneous nature of societies, three central points in the unitary conception of industrial society need reformulation. The three new sets of assumptions we suggest hardly amount to an integrated theory of industrial society, but their internal coherence and the wide spectrum of phenomena that they render comprehensible extend their explanatory range far beyond the traditional groups we set out to study.

First, societies should be conceptualized as by nature mixed and not unitary, as composed of economic and social groups reflecting different forms of economic organization, values, and modes of existence. Some groups will be those generated by the economic and social technologies and structures that are in the ascendancy in society; others will be survivors from periods when other forms of economic and social organization were dominant; others may be recent creations and yet have distinctly noneconomic origins.

The limits that economic pressures set for the range of values and activities that can be sustained within a society are so broad that they do not dictate any single relationship among groups. While economic structures may give an enormous social and political advantage to particular ones, it is the unusual case where this advantage has been translated into a situation of absolute domination. Rather, in conceptualizing the relationship among these fundamentally disparate groups, the notion of dominance explains only a part of the behavior that is critical. It is more useful to imagine that our societies are like the one that Marx describes in *The Eighteenth Brumaire of Louis Bonaparte:* composed of groups of very unequal power, with disparate assets and objectives, and with capabilities which, however considerable, can rarely be decisive when deployed alone. The presence and power of each group modify the terms on which the others can attain their objectives.

The mixed character of society is not a temporary, transitional condition but a permanent one. By this we do not mean that any given group or set of groups lasts forever. The numbers of peasants, shopkeepers, and artisans in Western Europe were far lower in 1978 than in 1958 and will be lower still in 1998. Some groups may disappear entirely. But what is significant is that through the heyday of industrial societies these groups maintain a significant presence and shape the patterns of development of even the most advanced segments of the economy. From this perspective, whether the peasants "ultimately" disappear is less consequential than the fact that in some advanced industrial societies their presence and power has led industrial groups to decisions in politics and in economics quite different than those that would have been made in the absence of the peasants, and the consequences of those choices may well outlive the peasantry. Groups disappear, and others once in the forefront of economic advance occupy the traditional sector. The mix within societies changes, but societies themselves do not shift from more mixed to more homogeneous composition.

The presence of groups, old and new, that are not directly generated by the central mechanisms of the economy reflects two processes that are as integral to social development as are the processes that make for integration and homogenization. First, the processes of industrialization and modernization that promote unity and integration in social structure also have perverse effects that reinforce and recreate heterogeneity. This phenomenon has been much studied in developing nations, where the emergence of strong ethnic groups, support for regional languages, and the reinforcement of parochial loyalties seem as typical products of increased communication and extended markets as do the emergence of societywide attachments and groupings. But the process is not restricted to societies in transition to modernity. In advanced industrial societies as well, the resurgence of regional ethnicity is one of the phenomena that demonstrate that modernity may create desires, frustrations, and aspirations which find satisfaction in "return" to preindustrial forms of association. In Edgar Morin's sense, modernization reinforces archaism.[14]

Secondly, the mixed character of societies is maintained and recreated by politics. In contrast to the view of the state in the unitary conceptions of industrial society, we conceive it not only as responding with more or less autonomy to the demands and needs of various social and economic groups but also as shaping social structure and economic activity. The state does not simply constrain, reward, and protect those groups it discovers before it. Instead, politics molds and channels social and economic processes. As the examples of Chapter 4 suggest, traditional groups that are losing out in the economy may retain political power sufficient to oblige the government to protect them against the competition of modern firms. The traditional sector in an industrial society may never have enough political clout to eliminate the modern sector but it may well have enough to prevent its own economic annihilation. The arrangements that preserve a certain space for traditional groups condition the evolution of the modern sector of society. By using politics to reshape social and economic change in ways that permit its continued survival and reproduction, the traditional sector can have a permanent impact on the economy and society.

What the state can preserve and create is of course limited by economic imperatives and by international competition. Automobiles cannot be produced by cottage industry, and no matter how much elites may fear the concentration of workers in large factories and desire the preservation of small, family-managed firms, if they wish to have cars manufactured in their society, they will have to accept large plants. They may decide against having an automobile industry, but they cannot decide against all heavy industry without consigning their nation to a subordinate role in the international system.

Within the limits set by technology and by the environment in which a society moves, there exists considerable latitude for institutional and social structural variation. The solutions that emerge in particular periods respond to economic and international exigencies and possibilities in ways that are shaped by the resources – material, ideal, political – available to given societies. This notion has been explored in the literature on industrialization in late-developing nations. As Gerschenkron has shown for Italy and Germany and Dore for Japan, the values, institutions, and social and economic technologies that accompanied industrialization in late-developing nations were significantly different from those of early-developing nations.[15] The requirements and opportunities of late industrialization impose certain similarities on all societies that develop after the first comers. Dore points out in his comparison of the British and Japanese industrial relations systems that the late development situation rewarded state intervention, bureaucratic organization, and large firms, and weighed against market-oriented institutions, gradual forms of development, and laissez-faire state policies.[16]

But the ways in which individual late-developing nations responded to the specific incentives and constraints inherent in the late development situation depended greatly on the resources and traditions available in their own national experience. As Dore shows, to explain the adoption of certain forms of trade union organization in Japan which were absent in Britain, we need to consider both the fact that such developments were rational responses in the situation the Japanese faced, industrializing at a later period than the British, *and* the fact that preexistent values and attitudes of workers and employers in Japan made such institutional development possible and desirable. The availability of different traditions, values, and institutions explains the diversity in the solutions that nations adopted in the course of industrialization and also accounts for the significant differences among industrial societies. Even when the reasons which once prompted recourse to a given institution disappear, the institution or practice itself remains and structures subsequent development.

The weight of preindustrial values and institutions in shaping industrial economies is not a phenomenon specific to late developers. Rather, even the patterns of early-developing capitalism in this light appear to be the product of historically based preferences for particular types of organization and authority. These values, then, shaped the societal response to technologically determined opportunities and imperatives. In this perspective, the British state can be seen as playing a critical role by rendering authoritative for all society the values of laissez-faire and individual enterprise held by some groups in it. The issue for all industrial societies would be to discover how the choices made in the course of industrialization are shaped and how they are generalized.

The third set of assumptions on which the perspective we suggest here departs from those implicit in the unitary conception of industrial societies have to do with the explanation of social change. The conventional theories we have discussed distinguish sharply between periods of transition and periods of maturity and between the modes of change specific to them. In periods of transition, the shifting bases of economic organization weaken the previously dominant classes and strengthen the hand of the rising classes, but no single

class can by itself exert a decisive influence on the resolution of conflicts, and therefore, alliances and outcomes are indeterminate. In
periods of maturity, in contrast, change is explained either as the
working out of processes or contradictions immanent in the economic
and social structure of industrialism or as the response to pressures in
the outside environment.

Drawing as sharp a distinction as these theories do between transitional and mature phases obscures the role in societies at *all stages*
of conflicts and alliances among heterogeneous groups. The decisive
struggles in advanced industrial societies are not only those in which
workers and business contend. Fights which do pit those two groups
against each other are not always resolved by the respective weights
of the two parties. The phenomena that Marxist and liberal theories
attribute to transitional stages are important, sometimes even decisive, in mature societies.

Social change should be conceptualized as resulting from interaction among potentially diverse and heterogeneous groups. The
examples in which change can be analyzed as a working out of tendencies immanent in technological evolution represent a limited set
of cases within a far wider range that includes conflicts and alliances
among groups generated by various social and economic cleavages.

In mature industrial societies as in transitional phases, the advanced motors of the economy are not steamrollers that flatten out the
terrain, producing a landscape whose features are entirely shaped by
specifically industrial social and economic forces. The landscape remains one of superimposed cleavages and groups. It follows that
when strains and shocks from the environment put stress on society,
they induce change by altering the internal balance of power among
social groups. Pressure from the outside does not weigh on societies
as "whole entities," as the systems analysts put it, but as differentiated and segmented entities. The environment is the source of
differential stresses and incentives for groups within society, and so
changes that come from the outside alter social equilibria by
strengthening the hands of some and weakening others. In contrast to
the unitary theories of society which conceive external stress as promoting change in society as a whole, in the perspective we suggest, it
is the unevenness of the impact of external pressure that accounts for
its transforming effects.

With respect to changes that arise from tension between the traditional and modern sectors, the nature of the process cannot be described simply as a lag effect, with modern groups dragging others in
their wake. The modern sector is deflected from its natural course and
transformed by having at different times to fight with, ally with, and

coexist with traditional groups. For example, in both France and Italy in the last decade, legislation has been passed to limit the expansion of supermarkets and protect small shops. The supermarkets thus blocked from seeking profits by massive increases in volume of sales will nonetheless continue to seek profits – with higher prices. The structures and management of the supermarkets will develop in ways that reflect the incentives and disincentives of operating in a protected arena. Confronted with a highly dispersed commercial network, industrial firms too, develop in quite different directions from those they might have pursued with a more concentrated system of mass distribution. When the protectionist legislation is overturned, as it probably will be, the modern firms that move out to capture the field will be enterprises with practices and structures different from what they might have been without the period of limitation by the traditional shops. The supermarket may win out over the small shop in the long run, but how this victory comes about may determine the shape of the modern sector.

Or consider the consequences for Italy of the massive transfer in recent years of economic activity from the large-scale, capital-intensive sector to the small-scale, labor-intensive sector (see Chapter 4). The possibility of regaining flexibility in the use of labor and reducing costs by subcontracting work to small firms has deflected investment and employment from the more advanced firms in the Italian economy to more technologically backward enterprises. It has undoubtedly contributed to the decline in investment. These transfers are likely to have consequences for the shape of the modern sector that far outlive the economic conjuncture that brought them about. For example, if, as seems likely, the current crisis of the European steel industry results in the collapse of certain companies, those in Italy that have the best chance of surviving are the small independent firms of Brescia, whose flexible use of labor and plant have allowed them to compete with the giants of the industry.[17] In the "long run," technological advance and industrial concentration may be decisive, but it is equally plausible that the shape of the long-term effects will reflect positions captured in the current round.

Indeed, arguments about long-term outcomes in contemporary societies mislead in so far as they are premised on the ultimate emergence of a "mature" form of industrial society with a unitary character and homogenous structures. If we imagine, instead, that industrial societies will always be composed of heterogeneous institutions and values and that these structures are discontinuous and segmental, then we must give up looking at the present as an incomplete version of the future. What this means for the present argument is that various coalitions among modern and traditional groups are not way stations to modernity but, rather, alternative variants of industrialism with potential for long life and resistance to change. The concept of an industrial society is then useful in so far as it specifies the constraints that industrialism, capitalism, and technological progress set on the range of variation in advanced industrial nations, but not useful as a model of the future toward which our societies move.

NOTES

1. Bert F. Hoselitz, "Interaction between Industrial and Pre-Industrial Stratification Systems," in N. Smelser and S. M. Lipset (eds.), *Social Structure and Mobility in Economic Development* (Chicago: Aldine, 1966), p. 191.
2. *Ibid.*, p. 193.
3. Gabriel Almond, "Introduction," in G. Almond and J. Coleman, *The Politics of the Developing Areas* (Princeton: Princeton University Press, 1960), pp. 24–5.
4. Karl Kautsky, *La question agraire* (Paris: 1900), p. 452, cited in Kostas Vergopoulos, "Capitalisme difforme (Le cas de l'agriculture dans le capitalisme)," in Samir Amin and Kostas Vergopoulos, *La question paysanne et le capitalisme* (Paris: Editions Anthropos-Idep, 1974).
5. Among the Marxist writings that have called the notion of the progressive universalization of capitalist structures and disappearance of "feudal remnants" into question, those of P. Ph. Rey, André Gunter Frank, A. Emmanuel as well as the previously cited Samir Amin and Kostas Vergopoulos are of particular importance in this context.
6. Vergopoulos, "Capitalisme difforme," p. 232. Trans. by S. Berger.
7. See on this point David Gold, Clarence Lo, and Erik Olin Wright, "Some Recent Developments in Marxist Theories of the State," *Monthly Review* (1975).
8. Samuel P. Huntington, "Postindustrial Politics: How Benign Will it Be?" *Comparative Politics, 7* (January 1974).
9. Daniel Bell, *The Coming of Post-Industrial Society* (New York: Basic Books, 1973), p. 13.
10. John Plamenatz, *German Marxism and Russian Communism* (London: Longmans, 1954). See also E. P. Thompson, *Whigs and Hunters* (New York: Pantheon, 1975), pp. 258–69.
11. Gabriel Almond and B. Bingham Powell, Jr., *Comparative Politics: A Developmental Approach* (Little Brown: Boston, 1966), pp. 13–14.
12. Joseph R. Gusfield, "Tradition and Modernity: Misplaced Polarities in the Study of Social Change," *American Journal of Sociology, 72* (January 1967), 351–62.

13. Julius H. Boeke, "Dualistic Economics," in *Indonesian Economics: The Concept of Duality in Theory and Policy* (Amsterdam: Royal Tropical Institute, 1961), text of lecture given in 1930.
14. Edgar Morin, *Commune en France* (Paris: Fayard, 1967), esp. pp. 61 and 276ff.
15. Alexander Gerschenkron, *Economic Backwardness in Historic Perspective*. Ronald Dore, *British Factory–Japanese Factory* (Berkeley: University of California Press, 1973).
16. *Ibid.*, pp. 415–17.
17. The best study of this is Paul Levenson, "The Metalworkers' Union and the Steel Industry in Brescia, since 1945," (Unpubl. undergraduate thesis, Harvard University, March 1979).

SELECTED BIBLIOGRAPHY ———

Amin, Samir, and Kostas Vergopoulos. *La question paysanne et le capitalisme*. Paris: Editions Anthropos-IDEP, 1974.

Averitt, Robert. *The Dual Economy*. New York: Norton, 1968.

Bagnasco, Arnaldo. *Tre Italie: la problematica territoriale dello sviluppo italiano*. Bologna: Il Mulino, 1977.

Bechhofer, Frank, and Brian Elliott, "Persistence and Change: the Petite Bourgeoisie in Industrial Society," *Archives européennes de sociologie, 17* (1976), no. 1.

Bell, Daniel. *The Coming of Post-Industrial Society*. New York: Basic Books, 1973.

Berger, Suzanne. "Uso politico e sopravvivenza dei ceti in declino," in F. L. Cavazza and S. R. Graubard, eds., *Il caso italiano*. Milan: Garzanti, 1974.

Boeke, Julius H. "Dualistic Economics," in *Indonesian Economics: The Concept of Duality in Theory and Policy*. Amsterdam: Royal Tropical Institute, 1961. (Text of a lecture given in 1930.)

Cain, Glen G. "The Challenge of Segmented Labor Market Theories to Orthodox Theory: A Survey," *Journal of Economic Literature, 14* (December 1979), no. 4.

Chandler, Alfred Dupont. *The Visible Hand: The Managerial Revolution in American Business*. Cambridge, Mass: Belknap Press, 1977.

Doeringer, Peter, and Michael J, Piore. *Internal Labor Markets and Manpower Analysis*. Lexington, Mass: Lexington Books, 1971.

Dore, Ronald. *British Factory – Japanese Factory*. Berkeley: University of California Press, 1973.

Edwards, Richard C., Michael Reich, and David M. Gordon, eds., *Labor Market Segmentation*. Lexington, Mass: D. C. Heath, 1973.

Gordon, David M. *Theories of Poverty and Underemployment*. Lexington, Mass: Lexington Books, 1973.

Hoselitz, Bert F. "Interaction between Industrial and Pre-Industrial Stratification Systems," in N. Smelser and S. M. Lipset, eds., *Social Structure and Mobility in Economic Development*. Chicago: Aldine, 1966.

150

Lutz, Vera. *Italy: A Study in Economic Development.* London: Oxford University Press, 1962.

Magaud, Jacques. "Vrais et faux salariés," *Sociologie du travail, 16* (January – March 1974), no. 1.

Mayer, Arno J. "The Lower Middle Class as Historical Problem," *Journal of Modern History, 47* (September 1975), no. 3.

Paci, Massimo. *Mercato del lavoro e classi sociali in Italia.* Bologna: Il Mulino, 1973.

Salvati, Michele. "L'origine della crisi in corso," *Quaderni piacentini, 11* (March 1972), no. 46.

Sylos-Labini, Paolo. *Saggio sulle classi sociali.* Bari: Laterza, 1975.

Wachter, Michael. "The Primary and Secondary Labor Market Mechanisms: A Critique of the Dual Approach," *Brookings Papers on Economic Activity* (1974), no. 3.

INDEX

accords de Grenelle, 33, 34, 39
Accornero, Aris, 123
AFL, 42, 45; see also unions
agriculture, see peasants, farmers
aliens, see migrant workers, foreign
Almond, Gabriel, 135, 140; see also
modernization (theory)
artisans, 91, 94, 105, 133, 134, 142;
in France, 95, 101, 114; political
mobilization of, 113; see also
firms, artisanal
automobile industry: assembly line
of, 19, 20, 60, 72; constraints of international competition on organization of production in, 144;
immigrant labor in, 57; in U.S., 42,
45, 68; subcontracting in, 37, 68,
107; see also Fiat
Averitt, Robert, 56

Bell, Daniel, 137
black workers, 17, 90, 99; compared
to white workers, 16; dual labor
market hypothesis to account for
situation of, 15; low propensity to
join unions, 47; relative powerlessness, 7; resistance to insecure
work, 48; see also, disadvantaged
workers; race
blue collar, see primary sector,
lower tier
Boeke, Julius, 4, 142
Bogotá, 6, 11, 27; see also Colombia

businessmen, small, 49, 50, 87, 91,
94, 105; defined in France, 125–
6n3; see also petty-bourgeoisie;
ownership, family

capital investment, 124; rigidities
introduced by, 103, 105
career advancement, see mobility
"catchall" parties, 115, 116, 117; see
also Christian Democrats; Gaullists
Catholicism, 116–17; and political
practice, 130n61
CGPME, 120
Chirac, Jacques, 117, 118, 122,
131n66
Christian Democrats, 29, 111, 112,
115, 118, 119, 122, 123; decline of
support for among Catholics,
116–17; see also "catchall" parties
CID-UNATI, see Nicoud
CIO, 42, 45; see also unions
class struggle: as explanation of origins of duality, 25; in France, 36;
in Italy, 29; in Marxist theory, 134
collective bargaining, 30, 45
Colombia, 3; see also Bogotá
comité d'entreprise, 35, 36
Communists (France), 113, 120; see
also Left (French); programme
commun
Communists (Italy), 29, 111, 112,

153